How to get what you Want

...and want what you get!

D0822139

How to get what you Want

...and want what you get!

12 Steps to Christian
Living at Its Best

WILLARD TATE

Christian Communications
P.O. Box 150
Nashville, TN 37202

Published by Christian Communications
A division of the Gospel Advocate Co.
P.O. Box 150, Nashville, TN 37202

ISBN 0-89225-356-8

Second Printing, 1990

This book is dedicated to our children,
Mark and Elisabeth, who have brought much joy,
happiness, and inspiration into our lives,
and to their lovely and loving families,
who make our lives much more abundant.

CONTENTS

INTRODUCTION

A lady named Eleanor Ritchey loved stray dogs. By itself, that's not so unusual. Two things, however, make her story a little different. For one thing, she loved strays so much that she kept 150 of them. And for another, she was an heir to the Quaker State Oil fortune, which made her a rich woman.

When Ms. Ritchey died in 1968, she willed $4.3 million to Auburn University's veterinary school, a most generous gift to further the education of future generations of animal doctors. But there was a catch. Her will stipulated that before the school could use a cent of the money for students or programs, it first had to be used to care for her pets for twenty years or until they all died, whichever came first.

In 1984, "Musketeer," the last of the 150 dogs, finally died. The vice chairman of the school's board of trustees said, "We ought to declare a school holiday," because by then the bequest had grown to $12 million!

Those of us who own and love pets can appreciate Ms. Ritchey's devotion to her dogs. But I think we'd agree that she had her priorities a little confused. For about sixteen years, the use of that money was tied up and withheld from the more-important purpose, the education of veterinarians. Stray dogs were kept in style at the expense of the training of future doctors.

The lesson for us in this story is that we need to keep in mind what's most important. There are many good things in life that we can be involved with, but let's never lose sight of that which is vital beyond all else. And while it's unusual to start a book with a disclaimer, I feel a need to begin this work with several. Let me explain.

First, I'm excited about the content of this book, "How to get what you want and want what you get." It grows out of a live seminar I give as often as I can because I've found the principles spelled out here to be life-changing in the most positive sense, both in my life and in the lives of others. I believe in these principles, and I'm convinced you'll be richly blessed if you also make them a part of your life. *However,* enjoying life—getting the most out of it you can—is *not* the most important thing. What is? Being rightly related to God through a personal, saving relationship with Jesus Christ in accordance with the Scriptures.

Having become God's children through adoption (see Gal. 4:4-7), we commit ourselves to self-denying service as required by the Savior: "Then he called the crowd to him along with his disciples and said: 'If anyone would come after me, he must deny himself and take up his cross and follow me. For whoever wants to save his life will lose it, but whoever loses his life for me and for the gospel will save it. What good is it for a man to gain the whole world, yet forfeit his soul?' " (Mk. 8:34-36).

That's what's most important, and I hope you've already made such a commitment of your life to Jesus Christ. If you have, you're ready to consider the principles in this book concerning how to make the most of this life with which we've been blessed.

Second, I want to make it clear that by no means am I the example of how to live or how to apply these truths. I have worked over the years to apply the lessons presented here from my own experience, and to the extent I've been able to do that, I've found them to be valid. (It is a poor teacher who tries to sell ideas that he doesn't believe in or use himself.)

As you read accounts in the chapters that follow of how I've used these principles please understand that I'm a fellow struggler. I don't always get things right; I make mistakes; I sometimes feel like a hypocrite because of teaching what I do not always practice!

The ideal example for us all is the Lord Jesus. His was the only perfect life. He came not only to save us from our sins, but also to show us how God would have us live. This is why the writer to the Hebrews told us, "Let us fix our eyes on Jesus, the author and perfecter of our faith" (Heb. 12:2). It's why Paul wrote, "Your attitude should be the same as that of Christ Jesus" (Php. 2:5). By following His example, we live as God intends.

With those qualifications in mind, let's remember that Jesus brings us more than just eternal life. He also wants us to have a new, fantastic *quality* of life—better than anything experienced by those outside His family. He described it like this: "The thief cometh not, but for to steal, and to kill, and to destroy: I am come that they might have life, and that they might have it more abundantly" (John 10:10, KJV).

In the following pages we'll explore how we can have more of that abundant life. I promise you that it can be life changing.

CHAPTER 1

Decide What You Want

The world makes way for the
man who knows where
he is going.

— *Ralph Waldo Emerson*

A man walked up to a gentleman standing on a street corner with a dog beside him and said, "Does your dog bite?"

"Nope," he answered.

So the first man reached out to pet the dog, and it growled and tried to chomp off his hand! He turned to the other man and said, "I thought you said your dog doesn't bite!"

The man looked down at the animal and said, "That ain't my dog."

It's vital that we ask the right questions in life. Asking the wrong ones could cost us a whole lot more than a hand. Life is full of important questions, including "Who is Jesus?" But the single most important question you and I will ever have to answer is "What do you really, really want?" In a sense, you see, it doesn't matter who Jesus is if we don't want Him. If we choose a life of independence from God, knowing the truth about Him won't help us.

If we never figure out what we want, we'll never enjoy the abundant life we all crave. We can know a lot of important things, but until we know just what we want, we'll never be satisfied.

In *Life Is Tremendous*, Charlie Jones tells of an old man who was being taken across a wide river by a young boy in a boat. As they were going along, the old man reached out and picked up a leaf that was floating by. He examined it,

1

then turned to the boy and said, "Son, do you know anything about biology?"

"No, Sir, I don't," the boy said.

"Well, boy, you've missed about 25 percent of your life," he replied.

A little later, the old man noticed a rock on the bottom of the boat. He picked it up and looked at it, and then he said, "Son, do you know anything about geology?"

"No, Sir, I don't."

"Well, boy, you've missed about 50 percent of your life."

It was growing late in the evening, and the old man was now looking at the stars as they came out. Finally, he turned again to the boy and said, "Son, do you know anything about astronomy?"

The boy bowed his head, ashamed, and said, "No, I don't."

"Well," the old man said, "you've missed about 75 percent of your life."

Just then the boy noticed that the dam above them had broken loose and that water was pouring through in torrents, hurtling toward them to dash their boat against the rocks and capsize them. He quickly turned to the old man and said, "Sir, do you know how to swim?"

"No," came the answer.

"Then you just lost your life," the boy shouted over the roar of the onrushing water.

Yes, we can know a lot and still not know the most important things, and the most important of all is the answer to "What do you really want?" We can have almost anything we want if we're willing to pay the price (this subject will be discussed in detail in the next chapter), so it's crucial that we be sure of what we want. And in this chapter, my goal is to help you answer that all-important question.

A Mission for Life

In his book *Why Settle for More and Miss the Best?*, author Tom Sine describes Mill Valley, California, a suburb of San Francisco. It's one of the most affluent towns in the United

States. Every home is worth a million dollars or more, and the driveways are dotted with Mercedes, Porsches, and BMWs. At Christmas, the living rooms look as if a department store had been dropped into them. The schools have the best, most modern equipment available. In short, the town lacks nothing money can buy.

But there's another side to the Mill Valley story. Those mansions house one of the highest rates of drug and alcohol abuse in the nation. Teen suicide is common. Families break up at an alarming rate.

Yes, you can get a lot of money if that's what you really want and you're willing to pay the price. But in deciding what you want in life, make sure your choice is one worthy of your efforts, one that will bring you true happiness and no bitterness with it. I'm not saying you can't be well off and happy, but make sure money and things and ambition don't possess you. By themselves, they won't ever produce a satisfying life.

Shortly after the suicide of comedian Freddie Prinz, a man familiar with many Hollywood celebrities was asked, "Do you know any other superstars in athletics or music or television or the movies who might also be in danger of deliberately taking their lives?"

After a moment's reflection, he answered, "I don't know anyone who is famous in these fields who is not in danger, because I don't know a single one who is happy."

While that's an obvious exaggeration, the point is that wealth and success are no guarantee of happiness or contentment, to say the least. Solomon made that clear thousands of years ago in the book of Ecclesiastes, where he told of trying everything the world has to offer and finding it all futile.

What we need first in deciding what we want is a mission in life—a vision of a life that's better than what we have now and that we can work toward all through our lives—a vision that's big enough and noble enough to be worthy of our best efforts. And once we settle on such a vision, it should be the guiding light on which we focus constantly. It should motivate us every day, occupy much of our thoughts every

day, and help us in sorting through the endless choices of
what we'll do every day.

All opportunities and all demands on our time and effort
are not equal. Some are more important than others. And
because we can really focus on only one thing at a time, our
success in life depends on whether we focus on the most
important things. When we lose that focus, we start to fail.
A good illustration of this is found in the movie "Rocky III."
The hero, Rocky Balboa, has won a boxing championship,
and then he decides to enjoy his success. He gets fat and
lazy in his big house. He forgets the work habits that made
him a champion. He loses his focus. Only when his manager
forces him back into workouts in a dark, smelly, rat-infested
gym does he regain his single-mindedness, his vision of
being a champion.

If you love to eat fattening foods but want to look good,
you have to choose one over the other. If you want to spend
time with your family but love television or to work all of
your waking hours, you have to choose one over the others.
If you want to build a business that meets human needs and
provides for your family but you like to sleep until noon,
you have to choose one over the other. Your mission in life
helps you make those choices.

What's a mission worthy of our best efforts, one that will
give the sense of purpose and meaning we all need, leading
to an abundant and satisfying life? Many of the details will
be different for each of us, but the starting point for us all
should be to glorify God. That's a purpose greater than any
other. Knowing that God loves us, cares for us, gave His
Son for us, and has heaven waiting for us, we respond in
submissive love, offering our lives to Him to use as He sees
fit. Proverbs 3:5-6 urges us, "Trust in the Lord with all your
heart and lean not on your own understanding; in all your
ways acknowledge him [put Him first], and he will make
your paths straight." Paul stated his commitment to such a
mission this way: "I consider everything a loss compared to
the surpassing greatness of knowing Christ Jesus my Lord. . . .
[O]ne thing I do: Forgetting what is behind and straining
toward what is ahead, I press on toward the goal to win the

prize for which God has called me heavenward in Christ Jesus" (Phil. 3:8,13-14).

Once you've settled on that as your overall mission in life, you can begin to shape a more specific vision that matches your individual dreams. Take an hour of quiet, uninterrupted time to think through what you really want in every area of your life—spiritual, your family, social, physical, and financial. Dream big, because we serve a big God. Most of us dream too small, greatly underestimating how much it's possible to accomplish in a lifetime. As I said before, there's almost no limit to what we can achieve if we first decide what we want and then pay the price to get it. So form that mental picture of a life that's better in all areas than what you have now and that's worth your best efforts to turn into reality.

Golden Goals

With a vision, or mission, to serve as your guiding light, the next step to clarify what you really want is to set some goals. In fact, good goals are priceless—having them is part of the wisdom that is "more profitable than silver and yields better returns than gold" (Pr. 3:14).

Why are goals so important? For one thing, it's impossible *not* to have goals of some kind. All of us have dominant thoughts or subjects that our minds constantly return to—possessions or positions we want, relationships we want to see changed, people we want to influence. And these things that we dwell on become our goals whether we recognize them as such or not. Do you have your eye on a new boat? a promotion at work? a place of leadership in your church? a young man or woman you think you'd like to marry? These are all different sorts of goals. I'm convinced God made us to be goal-setting and goal-seeking creatures, and we have goals all the time. Our goals will be better if we acknowledge that fact and take the time and effort to set our goals consciously and carefully.

Second, goals are important because of what they make of us in our pursuit of them. How we go about trying to

5

reach them, what we have to do in the process, and how we have to grow help to shape the people we become. A man whose only goal is wealth may become a cheat in order to obtain it. On the contrary, Solomon, whose goal was wisdom, became wealthy as well.

For example, as a basketball coach working to take a team to the national tournament, I put a lot of time and effort into *learning how people think, how to motivate them to better performance,* and *how to get a group of diverse people to work together* toward a common goal. Now, the achievement of my goal to go to the nationals was a great experience, but

---

God made us to be goal-seeking creatures.

---

much more important to my life were the skills and knowledge I learned—the better, more effective person I became—in the pursuit of my goal. You see, someone could steal the trophy—time itself has erased the memory of that trip for most other people—but nobody can take away the person I became in that pursuit.

Third, our goals reveal a lot about us. They tell us what's most valuable in our lives. As Emerson said, "Dreams [or goals] are the touchstones of our characters." Our goals determine how we spend our time and money, and how we spend our time and money tells the truest story about what kind of people we are.

Fourth, goals are important because they provide motivation. They give us a reason to get up in the morning, to go to work, to keep forging ahead even when the world seems set against us. They give that focus to our efforts that makes them seem worthwhile day in and day out.

Admiral Richard Byrd, the famous polar explorer, said that one day on his way to the North Pole, he stepped out of his cabin and instantly found himself in a blinding blizzard. The world was completely white with the driving snow—he couldn't even see his hand in front of his face. It was so bad that after just a few steps, he had lost all sense of direction. He knew that if he tried to find the cabin again and missed it, which would be easy to do under those conditions even though he was so close to it, he could freeze to death before he ever found his way back.

Fortunately, Byrd always carried a pole with him so he could jab the snow in front of him to see if there were any holes he might fall through. Operating entirely by feel, he drove this pole into the ground and tied one end of his scarf around it. Then he stepped out a short distance one way, always holding the other end of the scarf. He came back to the pole and went a little way in another direction. Four times he did this, each time finding nothing. Finally, on the fifth try, reaching out with his free hand, he located the cabin and made his way to safety.

Telling the story later, Byrd said, "There's no question that unless I'd had a central focus point to always come back to, I would have been lost." We, too, need a central focus point, a goal to guide and motivate us. And life's mission around which all of our goals must revolve is to glorify God if we are to enjoy a fulfilled, abundant life.

How to Set Goals

Recognizing the value of goals, how do we set good, specific, reachable goals? I suggest a four-step process. The first step is the one already mentioned—thinking through what you really want in each area of life to create your personal vision of a better future. This vision may be fairly general, and require a lifetime to fulfill.

Second, begin to narrow your focus. Write a list of the specific things you want to acquire, accomplish, become, see, do, have, or give away *in the next ten years*. Write them down—don't try to do this exercise in your head. There's something magic about putting pen to paper—it makes your wishes seem more real. At this point, write as fast as possible. Don't consider price.

Stay at this until you have a list of maybe fifty items. The longer the list the better. As a wise person said, "There is nothing to do but bury a man when the last of his dreams has died." If you don't have a long list of dreams, you're barely alive.

Third, look at your list and decide, as realistically as you can, which of those things you can achieve in the next twelve months if you really get after it—if you get up early and stay late, if you really turn it on. Put a star by those things. They're now your short-range goals.

Fourth, from among those short-range goals choose the five that are the most important, the most urgent, to you. Write them on a separate sheet of paper in the order of their priority to you. See if you have balance among them in terms of the major areas of life: spiritual, family, social, physical, financial and career. If there's imbalance or you've neglected one area, rethink this short list, and revise it if necessary. At this point, make sure the goals are stated in a form that's objectively measurable so you can know for sure when you've reach them—so many hours of Bible study each week, so many hours with your spouse or child, so many pages of that novel written, so many encouraging letters to friends written, or whatever.

Going through these four steps will take you about an hour, but if you do it seriously and honestly, it'll be one of the best things you ever do for yourself. It will show you the five most-important goals in your life, at least for this moment, letting you know what you most want to work on. You'll want to review this list in a year, and maybe even sooner if you sense your goals have changed. But these goals are the ones you want to pursue as of right now.

Reaching Your Goals

Now that you have specific, measurable, short-range goals to go after, how do you accomplish them? How do you turn the dreams into reality? That's what the whole first part of this book is about, but there is a six-step process that's effective in launching out after them.

First, you have to really sell yourself on your five goals. Begin by writing a paragraph about each. Discuss why you want it, what will happen when you achieve it, and how you'll feel about yourself. The idea is to give yourself reasons for pursuing this goal, and the more reasons you have, the more likely you are to reach your goals. You're also building the inner belief that you *can* accomplish what you want.

This is called fanning the flame of desire within you. We all have at least a little spark or glowing ember of desire to improve our lives and reach higher goals. If you fan that fire with reasons for putting forth the effort to pursue your goals, the flicker will gradually become a furnace of motivation.

Second, take a few minutes each morning to rewrite your five top goals. Grab pen and paper and go through the physical act of rewriting them. This helps to burn them into the subconscious—there's no better way to do it than to go over them day after day.

The Lord pointed to the effectiveness of this approach when He gave Israel the law through Moses and wanted to engrave His commands on their hearts and minds: "These commandments that I give you today are to be upon your hearts. . . . Talk about them when you sit at home and

---

Our life's mission is to glorify God.

---

when you walk along the road, when you lie down and when you get up" (Dt. 6:6-7). What the mind dwells on constantly, it remembers and accepts as reality.

Third, write each of your goals in affirmation form. An affirmation is a positive declaration of what you want to achieve. It needs to be written with three P's: it should be personal, positive, and present tense. Put your name in the affirmation, too. Let's suppose, for example, that one of your goals is to replace a critical attitude and critical comments toward your child with a more loving attitude and encouraging words. Your affirmation might go like this: "I, Mary Doe, have a much closer relationship with my son now that I focus on his potential and give him constant encouragement."

9

At the time you first write your affirmations, they may be far from reality. In the case of our example, you might not have said anything encouraging to your child in the last six months. But you affirm it because you want it to happen. The subconscious mind, you see, can't tell the difference between an affirmation grounded in reality and one grounded in desire, nor does it know time limits. So the more you affirm in your mind the things you want to be true, the more believable they'll become, and the closer to reality they'll grow.

Accordingly, write your affirmations on a card, and carry the card with you constantly in a convenient place like a shirt pocket. Then read the affirmations over and over throughout the day, as many times as possible.

A word of caution is needed at this point in the process— your dreams are very vulnerable. Criticism or ridicule from others could torpedo your efforts to make your goals seem reachable. So don't reveal your goals to anyone who will react negatively. Don't let someone else rob you of your commitment and enthusiasm. Keep your goals bottled up inside you, and let the excitement build.

Fourth, take a few minutes each morning (perhaps during breakfast or on a coffee break) to focus on your number one goal and write down twenty practical ideas of how you can go about achieving it. They may be small things, simple things, but make them positive moves toward the achievement of that goal.

Suppose, for example, that your goal is to become a regular, fruitful student of the Bible as measured by studying at least three hours each week. One idea for how to achieve it might be to read that magazine article you came across on how to start a quality Bible study program using just fifteen minutes a day. By itself, this idea won't take you to your goal, but it's a good start in the right direction.

After you write your list of twenty ideas, take action on one of them each day. If you stay with this program for at least thirty days, you'll really be fanning that flame of desire, and it will be getting hotter and bigger all the time.

Fifth, take ten or fifteen minutes each day to visualize the achieving of your goals. When you've reached them, how will you feel? Where will you be? Who will be with you? What sights, sounds, smells, tastes, and feelings will you experience? Let your mind play with the scene, using all your senses and emotions.

We've done this sort of thing all our lives. We call it daydreaming. I'm asking you to use it purposefully, to see your life the way you want it to be. Again, the mind can't tell the difference between a vividly imagined experience and a real one, so this is a further step in helping you believe your goals are reachable. This should also be fun!

Sixth, hang some kind of picture board at a spot in your bedroom where it will be the first thing you see in the morning and the last thing you see at night. Then cut pictures out of magazines and newspapers that reinforce your desire to reach your goals, and attach them to the board. These will further fan the flame within you, even during the night while your conscious mind rests.

We often do this naturally, especially young people. For example, when I was a college basketball coach, every time I went to the home of a top prospect to try to recruit him, I'd see posters up on his bedroom walls of Magic Johnson or Michael Jordan or Kareem Abdul-Jabbar. Those pictures reinforced his desire to become a great basketball player. And we can use pictures in the same effective way to reinforce our goals. Whatever our goals, as Christians we want to commit them to God and pray for His wisdom and power so that, when achieved, they will help us to honor and glorify Him.

A Personal Example

Now let me describe how I used this six-step process to reach one of my own goals. I first went through the goal-setting process explained earlier, and one of the goals I decided on, one that was very important to me, was to be a professional public speaker. At the time I set that goal, it was a long way from reality. I had done a little speaking in churches and civic clubs, and I was somewhat comfortable doing it, but it was sporadic, and certainly no one had ever paid me much.

First, I wrote my paragraph with reasons why I wanted to be a professional speaker, and began to sell myself on the goal. I rewrote the goal, along with others, every morning. I also did the daily exercise of listing twenty ideas about how to reach the goal, and one of the ideas on which I took action was to study with a man I'd heard about named Bill McGrain. He helped me write the affirmation: "I, Willard Tate, am an outstanding, successful, professional, fee-paid, public speaker now."

When Bill first gave me that, I can't tell you how embarrassed I was just to read it. I could hardly say it out loud, even to myself. It was so unbelievable! But I began reading it to myself over and over, timidly.

As soon as I started, I began hearing those little inner voices. (Do you know the ones I mean?) I'd say, "I'm an outstanding professional speaker," and the voices would say, "You've never been outstanding at anything. You're not a professional speaker. Who are you fooling? You're just lying to yourself!" When I'd say, "I'm a fee-paid speaker," the voices would laugh at me and say, "Who's going to pay you? Nobody has ever paid you to speak. Why should they?"

In spite of the voices and my embarrassment, however, I kept repeating the affirmation. And guess what happened. Slowly, it became more believable, and the voices grew quieter and came less often. I began saying it with more feeling and authority. I even started to say it out loud when I was jogging or in the car by myself. (I still couldn't say it to my wife.) I would emphasize every word, and I found myself getting genuinely excited about the goal, even though it wasn't actually happening yet.

Other things I did to reach the goal included joining the National Speakers Association, writing some speeches, subscribing to some magazines, and going to seminars. I also visualized myself actually standing on stage in front of a huge crowd. I saw my hands and feet and gestures. I felt my muscles moving, heard the sounds and smelled the smells inside the auditorium, and felt the roar of the standing ovation and the pats on the back at the end. I experienced all the emotions I would have if it were real. I put up my picture board, too, using photos of great speakers like Paul Harvey, Zig Ziglar, and Bob Richards to inspire me.

At first I had no audiences for the speeches I wrote. But slowly, I'd get an engagement here, another one there. And I became a different speaker from the one I'd been before, and each appointment generated another somewhere else. The first thing I knew, I was doing a lot of speaking.

About a year after starting the process, I found myself giving a speech at a national sales convention in Hot Springs, Arkansas. There was a number of other speakers on the program, all of them top-notch, well-paid people. After my speech, the audience gave me a standing ovation that seemed to last fifteen minutes. (Now you know I'm dreaming!) I remember standing there with tears running down my cheeks, thinking back to a year earlier, when I couldn't even say my goal out loud, and now it was all coming true. I was like the old boy who said, "I had never seen an English teacher, and now I are one!" Today I get more invitations to speak than I can accept. And it all began with setting a goal and fanning the flame of desire and believability—when you believe something, it *can* happen!

If I could read your mind right now, you might be saying, "Oh, come on, Willard. I don't have time to rewrite goals and write down twenty ideas and visualize and recite affirmations every day." But the fact is, you're already doing a lot of those things. You're telling yourself things about yourself all the time, whether positive or negative. You're visualizing some kind of future for yourself. You have some goals you're pursuing, however vague or meaningful they may be. So all I'm asking is that you do these things in a systematic way, and that you use the process of self-enhancement rather than self-destruction.

When you fan the fire of desire and motivation, you begin to believe in your goals, others begin to believe them, and they start to become reality. I know the process works. It worked for me and it will work for you, too.

Chapter Insights

1. Why are personal goals so important? Are there people who have no goals of any kind?
2. What are some questions we all have to answer?
3. What could you do if you are not sure what your life's goals should be? Who could offer you guidance?
4. Mr. Tate said, "What the mind dwells on constantly, it remembers and accepts as reality." What does your mind usually dwell on? How helpful are these thoughts? Do they build you up?
5. Read Philippians 4:8. What are some good things your mind should dwell on?

CHAPTER 2

Be Willing to Pay the Price

*Nothing of a worthwhile,
durable nature
in the world has been produced
without sweat.*

— *Herbert Lockyer*

It's amazing what you can do if you're willing to pay the price. In high school, I had shown little ability to study well, and even less desire. As a result, I didn't know an adverb from an adenoid. But I knew that if I ever wanted to make anything of myself in this life, I needed to get a college education. I was like the guy who said he used to dream of going to college. "When was that?" his friend asked.

"When I was sleeping through my high school classes," he answered.

To say I found college challenging would be a major understatement. I had poor academic skills, I felt terribly ill prepared, and I was scared to death. But I had one big thing going for me that made a world of difference: I was willing to pay the price to succeed. And in my senior year at Auburn University, I made straight A's. (I don't say that to brag but to show you what's possible. If I could do it, *anybody* could!)

What price did I have to pay? It began with a commitment to study as long as it took to understand the material. Many of my college students today think they've paid their dues and should have mastery of a subject after reading through an assignment just once. But it doesn't usually work that way, and it certainly didn't for me. I sometimes had to read an assignment over four or five times.

I also asked my teachers for help. I studied with good students. To improve my spelling, I humbled myself to listen to first-grade tapes. I also humbled myself to ask for my wife's help, and she taught me how to study and stick with it. My ego was big, and my ignorance was even bigger, but I was determined to change that. I got up at 3 A.M., too, to study for tests.

Let me digress a little here and give Bobbie a big pat on the back. She helped me to get through college, as many wives have, by typing my papers. (She corrected my grammar, spelling, etc.!) She also took care of our kids and the house AND worked outside the home to help support us. When my confidence and dedication to study sagged, she was there to pick me up and get me going again. If any wife ever earned her Ph.T. (Putting Hubby Through) degree and her husband's undying thanks, it is Bobbie.

One time I was taking physics—or maybe I should say it was taking me. Despite all my hard work, I failed the first two tests. That's when I came home and told my wife that I thought I'd just drop the course because I didn't think I could pass. She told me something then that I needed to hear and that I've never forgotten: "You are already enrolled and have come this far; you will have an F if you quit, so you have nothing to lose by trying." I eventually earned a C for the course. Today I'm prouder of that C than I am of a lot of the A's I earned, because it's given me the motivation I needed to pay the price on many occasions.

In fact, the principle Bobbie helped me learn on that occasion is so important that I teach it to my students. If you have nothing to lose and everything to gain, by all means *try*. The reverse is also true: *If you have everything to lose and nothing to gain, by all means* don't!

How Bad Do You Want It?

One of the keys to my success in college was that I wanted it badly enough to pay the price in all its forms—the time, the money, the effort, the humility. I knew that the price would be high (I didn't know how high—and that was probably good,) but with my wife's blessing and help, I determined to pay it. The longer I live, the more convinced I become that you can have *whatever* you want if you're willing to pay the price.

This is why it's so important to determine just what you want, as discussed in the preceding chapter. We all could make long wish lists of things we want, but with most of the things on our lists, our desire is only strong enough that we'd accept them if they came floating by. That's about the limit of the effort we'll put forth to get them. So we must set priorities on our wants and devote ourselves to the ones that really matter.

When I play golf and my ball lands in the rough or in a sand trap, as it often does, I say to myself and my playing partners, "Man, I wish I weren't here. I want to play some good golf like those pros on TV!" And you know, if I took some lessons and practiced an hour a day, my golf game would get a whole lot better. In a few months, my ball would be landing in the fairways and on the greens most of the time instead of in the rough. But as much as I'd like to play good golf, I don't want to badly enough to pay the price. With all the other things I'm doing that I enjoy and that I think are productive, I just can't afford the time, money, and effort that improving my golf game would cost.

Playing the five-string banjo is something else I enjoy and would like to do much better. (I'm not very good, but I smile a lot, so I call it pickin' and grinnin'!) Sometimes I use it in programs, and that's the only time I play; I practice very little. Here again, I'm sure that with lessons and practice, I could get a lot better. But on my list of priorities, becoming a top-notch banjo player isn't very high. You could say that I play the banjo just about as well as I want to. (That might sound strange if you heard me play!) If I really wanted to play better, I'd be willing to pay the price required.

A woman ran up to the great violinist Fritz Kreisler one time after a concert and said to him, "I would give my life to play as beautifully as you."

He replied, "I did."

Now, it's important that we understand the price of something to determine whether we're willing and able to pay it *before* we start. Otherwise we set ourselves up for frustration and disappointment. I've decided not to even begin the process of seriously improving my golf and banjo playing because I know the price is higher than I want to pay. Jesus taught more than two thousand years ago: "Suppose one of you wants to build a tower. Will he not first sit down and estimate the cost to see if he has enough money [or desire, we might add] to complete it? For if he lays the foundation and is not able to finish it, everyone who sees it will ridicule him" (Lk. 14:28-29).

Willing to Work

Having decided to pay the price, we have to dig in and actually do the work. We human beings are lazy by nature, and we tend to look for the easy way to get things done. We're expert at doing a job just well enough to get by. But in my experience, the easier we are on ourselves, the harder the world and the system seem to be on us. And the harder we are on ourselves, the easier the world and the system seem to be on us. To put it another way, we have to pay *in advance* for the good things in life, but we pay *later* for the easy way. We need the attitude of George Bernard Shaw when he said, "When I was young I observed that nine out of ten things I did were failures, so I did ten times more work."

It's easy to talk about what we want to do without ever taking action. You probably know at least one person who has always talked about a major goal like spending more time with his children or starting his own business, yet for one reason after another he's never taken the necessary steps to make it happen. An old Chinese proverb says a journey of a thousand miles begins with a single step, and until we get off our seats and take that first step, we'll never achieve a thing.

Now, at this point it's easy to fall into a trap of ignorance and excuses like my students who think they ought to make an A just because they read the assignment once. And when that happens, we never achieve our goals, never fulfill our potential. On the other hand, if we first *understand ourselves* and then *manage ourselves*, we're more than likely to succeed. In fact, I'd say that 80 percent of what we achieve, whether it's failure or success, relates to these two factors.

What do I mean by "understanding ourselves"? I mean the ability to look at ourselves honestly and know if we're really willing to pay the price and if we are in fact paying it. Some students who are doing poorly in my class whine that they "read the assignments," as if that simple fact excuses them from the poor results of their tests. They've deceived themselves into thinking that because they put forth a *little* effort, they should be rewarded with good grades. If they could look at themselves honestly and understand, they'd see they're not really willing to pay the price of

---

The tougher we are on ourselves,
the easier life becomes.
The easier we are on ourselves,
the tougher life becomes.

---

success, and they're not putting out the kind of effort success demands. They're much better at making excuses than they are at paying the price to master the material in a college course.

Benjamin Franklin wisely observed, "Well done is better than well said." Life doesn't generally accept or reward excuses. It honors results. So my students—or anyone who's not doing as well as he'd like—need to look objectively at their level of desire and work, and decide how much more they need to do to get from where they are to where they want to be. If that means reading an assignment through four or five times before they're confident they understand it, that's what they should be prepared to do. We have to understand ourselves relative to our willingness to work.

Then we have to manage ourselves—make ourselves do the work. It's called self-discipline, and boy is it hard if we're not in the habit! Jack Paar, the television personality, spoke for most of us when he said, "It seems to me that my whole life has been one long obstacle course, with me as the chief obstacle."

Compare the people you know, including yourself, to a member of the music faculty at the college where I teach. He's a pianist, and he told me one time that during the school year, in addition to carrying a full teaching load, he tries to practice the piano 2 or 3 hours every day—except on weekends. Then he practices 4 or 5 hours every day. He added that during some holidays he would get in 6 to 8 hours daily. And finally he mentioned that in preparation for his last concert, he had practiced the music for 1,200 hours!

Can you imagine what you and I could achieve in our workplaces, our homes, our hobbies if we put that kind of time and effort into them? No wonder most of us get so little out of life—we give so little. We're like the hound dog who was sitting in a country store in the Ozarks and howling his head off the way only hounds can. A stranger came in and said to the storekeeper, "What's the matter with that dog?"

"Oh, he's sitting on a cocklebur," was the answer.

"Why doesn't he get off?" the stranger asked.

"He'd rather holler than move," came the reply.

That's the way of so many of us. We'd rather complain and gripe and criticize and condemn than put forth any effort. But that won't get the job done. Backbone beats wishbone every time! No sweat, no sweet.

I've had the privilege to speak a number of times in Yosemite, California, one of God's most beautiful creations. There are some rock peaks there that are popular with climbers, and time and again as my wife and I have watched those men climb, we've been amazed by their concentration and effort. I've concluded that rock climbing is probably more like life than any other sport.

Tom Callanan, a climber, explains that when you climb in what's known as zone 3, you enter another reality where the smallest holes become like ledges, the slightest sounds clap like thunder, and the longest climb is a timeless interlude, a thin scene between life and death. When you're climbing the face of a huge rock or cliff, Tom says there are no time outs, there are no substitutions, and quitting is not an option. Once you're up there, only you can get you off. Further, it's often the case that the only way out is to keep going up to the top. So if up is impossible, *you had better learn to do the impossible, and fast.* Most of us have never lived on that kind of plane and given that kind of effort, so we've also never known the kind of joy it brings. But we can, and we must if we want to achieve worthwhile goals.

The Value of Work

No doubt one key to our willingness to pay the price in work is our *attitude* toward work. As I said earlier, most of us look for the easy way to do what we must. We try to do as little as necessary to get by. In short, we avoid work as much as possible; we clearly don't like it! But I've learned that it makes a lot more sense to *love* our work and give it our very best effort.

For one thing, we need to recognize that work is a reward, a blessing, from God. Some Christians have gotten the mistaken idea that work is a part of the curse resulting from Adam and Eve's fall into sin, recorded in Genesis 3. But if we look back in Genesis 2:15, we see that God appointed Adam to tend the Garden of Eden *before* the Fall. This work as a gardener was given to man as part of God's plan for the perfect, sinless world He had created. In His judgment of Adam and Eve's sin, God said their work would forever after be made difficult by thorns and thistles, but He never said that work itself was a curse. Just the opposite.

In fact, I like to think of my work as my best friend in some ways. For example, I love it as a friend because it allows me to do something very important—provide food, clothing, and shelter for myself and my family. There's not much in my life that's more important to me than that, and my work lets me meet that need. The least I can do is return some love to the thing that feeds me.

I also love my work because it lets me do something I really enjoy. I love to teach college students, and I love to speak in seminars. I get high on the interaction with an audience. I thrill to see the nods and smiles that indicate I'm getting through to people and giving them something that's going to improve their lives. I can't imagine anything I'd rather do. If I had to, I'd probably pay somebody for the privilege of doing what I do; but instead, people pay me. What a concept! Other people love to plan things and see them take shape—they become engineers and architects and designers. Others love to see sickness defeated and people made well—they become doctors and nurses and lab technicians and medical researchers. Still others love to see people enjoy the comfort and satisfaction of owning their own homes, so they become builders and real estate agents and bankers.

My point is that if we choose our careers wisely, we can find jobs that allow us to do the things we enjoy most. The happiest people in the world are the ones who are getting paid to do the things they love. The unhappiest people, on the other hand, are the ones stuck in jobs they don't like. Author Srully Blotnick, in his book *Getting Rich Your Own Way*, said that in studying how people become millionaires, he concluded that the biggest factor is that they love what they're doing. Now, we won't all become millionaires by loving our work, but we *will* be rich in the way that matters most—in self-esteem, in satisfaction, in feeling that the many hours we put into our work are well spent.

The story of Eddie Rickenbacker, the World War I flying ace, illustrates the value of finding a work you can love and pursuing it as a satisfying career. Born in Columbus, Ohio, in 1890 as the third of eight children, he had to quit school at age eleven to help his family with expenses. He got a full-time job and stayed with it until age fifteen, when he developed an interest in cars and went to work in a garage. But he knew he needed more education, so he subscribed to correspondence courses on automobiles. And night after night, after a long day's work in the garage, he would study at his kitchen table under the kerosene light.

Rickenbacker already knew where he wanted to work when he was prepared—the Frayer Miller car company in Columbus. When the day came that he felt ready, he walked into the plant and right up to Lee Frayer, who had his head under a car hood. When Frayer saw Eddie he asked what he could do for him, and Eddie answered, "I just thought I would tell you that I am coming to work here tomorrow morning."

"Oh, who hired you?" Frayer said.

"Nobody yet," said Eddie, "but I'll be on the job in the morning, and if I'm not worth anything, you can fire me."

What an attitude! And sure enough, Rickenbacker showed up early the next morning, before even Frayer had arrived. Looking around, Eddie noticed the floor was thick with metal shavings, dust, and grease. So he found a broom and shovel and started cleaning the shop. You can guess the rest of the story. And Eddie eventually combined his love of engines with his love of flying and founded Eastern Airlines.

I once had a student named Coyt Dunlap with a similar love of work. He determined he wanted a career in banking, so while still a student he went to the bank he liked and got the job cutting their grass. Then he started showing up just to run errands for them. You can finish this story, too. Today he's a vice president at that bank.

Then, too, I love my work because it gives me the chance to develop God-given talents. I want to keep growing, developing, learning to do the things I enjoy even better,

---

If you never do more than you get paid for, you will never get paid for more than you do.

---

and my work is the arena where I do that. To stop growing is to stagnate and die. If we can find at least one thing we can do well and make a career out of it, continually building on our skills, it also does wonders for our sense of worth and self-esteem. Ron Willingham said, "The more you develop your talents, the better you will like yourself."

Each of us can do at least one thing well if we will discover what it is and work to develop it. We also do our children a great service if we help them discover their talents and learn to work so they can make the most of their gifts.

Then finally, I love my work because it's the best therapy I know. There's no better medicine for a soul in distress than to throw yourself into work. Why? Because it's impossible to concentrate on your work and worry at the same time. As you get wrapped up in the work, your worries fade into the background; the world seems to take on a brighter outlook. I've experienced this many times when working on a project or preparing a speech. My wife has often thrown herself into housework as a way of dealing with sorrow or disappointment. It makes a big difference.

Dean Briggs put it this way: "Do your work and a little more, that little more which is worth all the rest. And if you suffer, as you must, and if you doubt, as you must, do your work. Put your heart into it and the sky will clear, and then out of your very doubt and suffering will be born the supreme joy of life."

Paying the Price in Patience

My friend Wimp Sanderson illustrates another important part of paying the price, and that's knowing how long success takes and being willing to wait. Oh, this is hard! When we know what we want, we want it right away. Instant gratification—that's what life is all about, or so we tend to think. That's what the commercials and the credit card companies tell us. But Wimp knew better.

Wimp is a college basketball coach and he loves the game. For a long time he wanted to be the head coach at the University of Alabama, and for a long time he had to wait for his chance. In fact, he spent something like *twenty-two years* as an assistant coach there before he got the top spot. He worked hard and well under a number of other coaches until he was given the job, but he knew what he wanted and was willing to pay the price of patience. Most of us would have given up long before that and gone in search of greener pastures, but Wimp was wise, and both he and the school have been rewarded for his patience.

Almost anything of value takes time to develop, whether it's job skills or family relationships or the building of prosperity. Accepting that, working with that, calculating realistically how long something will take if it's done well, and resisting the lure of the easy way are part of paying the price of success.

Partnership with God

Finally, it is much easier to pay the price for something worthwhile if we see ourselves working in partnership with God. This gives us "the big picture," the assurance that we're serving Him by making a contribution to our fellow man.

There were three men working on a building. A passerby asked the first one, "What are you doing?"

"I'm making $7 an hour," he said.

The passerby moved on to the second workman and asked, "What are you doing?"

"I'm laying bricks to put up this building," he said.

Then the passerby went to the third workman and repeated his question.

"Why, I'm building a great cathedral for the glory of God," he answered.

You can imagine which man was paying the price and reaping rewards that go far beyond a paycheck.

I heard of a coal miner with a similar attitude. One time someone said he felt sorry for the miner, who had to work in dark, dirty tunnels under the ground. "Oh, I don't think you understand," the miner said, holding out a lump of coal. "This is not just a lump of coal. This is light, heat, and power. This will provide light for city streets, heat to warm a house, and power to run a train."

This kind of attitude says, "I'm not working for money. I'm improving the quality of life. I'm giving something back, helping to make the world a better place than I found it. I'm pleasing God by serving others in love." And with that perspective, our work takes on great dignity, priceless value. This was the thought Paul had in mind when he wrote, "Whatever you do, work at it with all your heart, as working for the Lord, not for men, since you know that you will receive an inheritance from the Lord as a reward. It is the Lord Christ you are serving" (Col. 3:23-24).

For this reason, I believe Christians ought to be better workers than non-Christians. I believe we ought to make all we can (see, e.g., Mt. 25:14-30; Eph. 4:28), save all we can (see Jn. 6:12), and certainly give all we can.

But paying the price in partnership with God also has to include paying a spiritual price of self-denial. Our commitment in all we do must be to follow the leading of our King, whatever that may require of us. Jesus said, "If anyone would come after me, he must deny himself and take up his cross and follow me" (Mt. 16:24). The apostle Paul commanded us in Romans 12:1, "Therefore, I urge you, brothers, in view of God's mercy, to offer your bodies as living sacrifices, holy and pleasing to God—this is your spiritual act of worship."

Now, this is not a call to the shut-away life of a monk. God is active in the world, and He wants His people to be active as well, making the world a better place, working hard, striving for spiritual growth, reaching out in love. We want to be ready to die for Him, but the greater challenge is to *live* for Him, walking in the light as He is in the light (1 Jn. 1:6-7), standing fast in the spiritual conflict clad in the whole armor of God (Eph. 6:10-11). And when we do, we'll understand what Henry Ward Beecher meant when he said, "Victories that are cheap are cheap. Those only are worth having which come as a result of hard fighting."

The ideas of partnership with God and paying the price spiritually are summed up beautifully in a piece I came across titled "The Disciple's Charge":

> I'm a part of the fellowship of the unashamed. The die has been cast. I have stepped over the line. The decision has been made. I'm a disciple of His. I won't look back, let up, slow down, back away, or be still.
>
> My past is redeemed, my present makes sense, my future is secure. I am finished. I'm done with low living, sight walking, small planning, smooth knees, colorless dreams, tame visions, mundane talking, chintzy giving, or dwarf goals.
>
> I no longer need pre-eminence, prosperity, position, promotions, platitudes, or popularity. I don't have to be right, first,

tops, recognized, praised, regarded, or rewarded. I now live by presence, lean by faith, walk by patience, lift by prayer, and labor by power.

My face is set, my gait is fast, my goal is heaven, my road is narrow, my way is rough, my companions few, my God reliable, my mission clear.

I cannot be bought, compromised, detoured, lured away, turned back, deluded, or delayed. I will not flinch in the face of sacrifice, hesitate in the presence of adversity, meander in the maze of mediocrity!

I won't give up, shut up, let up until I have stayed up, stored up, prayed up, paid up, preached up for the cause of Christ. I am a disciple of Jesus. I must go till He comes, give till I drop, preach till all know, and work till He stops me. And when He comes for His own, He will have no problem recognizing me—my colors will be clear!

—(Author unknown)

Chapter Insights

1. Everyone has a "hope chest" of sorts or a "wish list." How much time and effort are you actually putting into making your hopes and dreams come true?
2. Think of an area of your life with which you are dissatisfied. Being honest with yourself, how much effort are you actually putting into improving it?
3. What might be included in paying the price to get what you want?
4. How long are you willing to wait for success? Would success be more likely if you were more patient? Why?
5. Read Ecclesiastes 3:1. What does it suggest about the timing of getting what you want?

CHAPTER 3

Ask for It

*If you are reluctant to ask the
way, you will be lost.*

— *Malay proverb*

When I was coaching college basketball, our big goal each
year was to get to the NAIA national tournament in Kansas
City at the end of the season, and I had the good fortune
to accomplish that once in my career. After I quit coaching
(some years ago now), my wife and I often discussed our
desire to go back there some time as spectators. We love the
game and just wanted to sit and soak up basketball from
9:30 in the morning until 12:30 at night, eating chocolate
malts and roasted peanuts. Well, we did that recently, and
we had a marvelous time.

We noticed one night that the ushers were passing out
little souvenir basketballs to the children who came. Bobbie
saw them and said, "Willard, I've got to have one of those
NAIA basketballs for each of my grandkids." (We have three
wonderful grandchildren.)

"I don't know any way to get them," I said, "but if you
know me, you know I'll ask," so I talked to several people
who had the small basketballs, and I also asked the ushers.

"Oh, no, you can't buy them," they all said. "They're a
gift to children accompanied by their parents."

I had about given up on getting any basketballs, but
Bobbie wouldn't take no for an answer, so I kept asking and
kept asking. Finally I found a tournament official in a back
room and told him my story. "I've got three grandchildren,"
I said, "and my wife won't go back to Texas with me if I

28

don't have three of those souvenir balls. How can I get them?''

At first he said, "You can't." Then he said, "Well, I'll tell you what. Come back here about 11:00 tonight. I've got a few spares that I kept back just in case some were bad, and if we don't need them, I'll let you have those."

I walked back in there at about 11:00, and sure enough, they had two basketballs for me which they *gave* me! I needed another, but they didn't have any more. As we were about to leave the arena, however, we saw some older boys who had the miniature balls. I asked them if they knew anyone who would want to sell a souvenir ball, and one of them offered me his basketball for five dollars, and I gave him ten. (The other boy was upset that he didn't get to sell his!)

When we walked out that night, we had our three basketballs, simply because I wouldn't quit. I kept asking. There was no secret to it, just the willingness to ask and ask until I found the right people and got the answer I wanted.

Just Ask

One of the keys to getting what we want, I've found both in the Bible and in my experience, is just to ask. It's that simple, yet we often find it difficult to do.

God has made some amazing promises in this regard. In Matthew 7:7, Jesus said, "Ask and it will be given to you; seek and you will find; knock and the door will be opened to you." That's a pretty strong statement, and there are others like it. In Matthew 18:19, He said, "Again, I tell you that if two of you on earth agree about anything you ask for, it will be done for you by my Father in heaven." If that weren't enough, Jesus also said in John 15:7, "If you remain in me and my words remain in you, ask whatever you wish, and it will be given you." Finally, although there are many other passages which teach the same, we have this promise from the apostle John: "This is the confidence we have in approaching God: that if we ask anything according to his will, he hears us. And if we know that he hears us—whatever

we ask—we know that we have what we asked of him"
(1 Jn. 5:14-15).

Those are God's promises, God's statements, not mine. I
didn't write the formula. And He, the One who made us
and knows us best, said the best way to get what you want
is to ask for it. That's how you get the most that's gettable.

Let's not misunderstand God's words, however. Just because we ask doesn't mean we're going to get $100,000-a-year
jobs or Mercedes cars to drive. Such promises have to be
interpreted in the context of the whole Bible, and I don't see
from that perspective that God is very concerned about
making us rich materially. As the wisest man who ever lived
said, "Better a little with the fear of the Lord than great
wealth with turmoil" (Pr. 15:16). But God *is* extremely
interested in blessing us spiritually, giving us peace, joy,
contentment, wisdom, and the knowledge of how to love.
Those are true riches, the building blocks of an abundant life.
And God says these things are available without limit if
we'll only ask.

Truths About Asking

There are at least six truths I've learned about asking over
the years. They summarize why asking is so effective. First,
asking is the beginning of receiving. It's as if it pushes all our
emotional and mental buttons. Asking works with other
people as well as with God.

Nearly all of us have been trained from the age when we
were "knee high to a duck" (that's pretty small) to be nice
to people, to be helpful, to do what we're asked, especially
if we're asked politely. Furthermore, we like to help—it gives
us a chance to use our knowledge and talents, and it feels
good.

On the other hand, it's usually the case that if we don't
ask, we don't receive. In my seven years as basketball coach
at Abilene Christian University, I never lost a player to
academic ineligibility. This success didn't come easily, however. I went out of my way to keep tabs on my players, to

check on whether they were attending classes, how they were doing on tests, and so on.

More than once I got back reports from professors saying a player had flunked his last test. And often when I got such a report, the professor would add this kind of comment: "I believe Joe doesn't know how to study. If you'll get him to come by and see me during office hours, I'll be happy to work with him and see if I can help." So I'd call Joe into my office, and the conversation would typically go something like this:

"Joe, how's it going with you?"

"Everything's fine, Coach."

Then I'd ask about his roommate, his church involvement, his girlfriend, slowly working my way around to his academics. Finally I'd start to probe there, asking him about each class and how he was doing. You won't believe what Joe would say when I asked about the class in which he had just flunked a test. "Fine. Doing just fine."

How do you explain that? Here the kid was drowning academically, and I was offering him a life raft to save his scholarship and his college career, but he'd insist everything was fine. So I'd press on and say, "Joe, that's interesting, because I just got a note from the professor saying you flunked the last test."

He'd then try to win an Oscar, putting on the biggest act you've ever seen. "Oh, really? I can't believe it! I thought I did well on that test."

Eventually I'd get him to come clean and admit he was struggling. Then I'd explain that the professor was willing to help if Joe would go to see him during office hours. I'd also take the initiative to make the appointment and show Joe where the professor's office was. If the professor was free only during basketball practice, I'd excuse Joe from practice so he could go get the help he needed.

The day after the appointment, I'd see Joe at practice and ask how his session with the professor went. And do you know what I heard more times than you'd believe? *Joe didn't go.* Despite the fact that his scholarship was on the line and I had made all the arrangements for him, Joe would not take advantage of the help that was there for the asking. And then I made sure that he went the next day.

I've found that help is available in so many areas, and, people in general want to help. But it has to begin with asking.

The second thing I've learned follows right on the heels of the first: *receiving is not the problem; failing to ask is.* If we ask God for the blessings He wants to give us, if we ask others politely for help, or if we set goals and work for them, receiving is almost automatic. I'm amazed when I look back at the major goals I set ten and fifteen years ago and realize I've already surpassed them. It's scary! But I want you to

---

Receiving begins by asking.

---

get excited about what's possible. Believe me, receiving is not the problem. Failing to ask, like Joe's refusal to ask for academic help, is what cuts off the flow of getting what you want even before it begins.

In John 16, Jesus was preparing His disciples for His death and later ascension into heaven, and in verse 5 He said, "Now I am going to him who sent me, yet none of you asks me, 'Where are you going?' " I see a bit of an indictment in that statement, as though He wanted them to ask questions, to be more inquisitive about the Father and about heaven. By their failure to ask, they didn't receive all He could have told them.

Even today, we can't get people to ask the right questions or the right people. Students aren't interested enough to ask the right questions in class. Employers won't ask the right questions about how to do the job better or how to market the product more effectively. People in the pews gossip among themselves but don't ask the leaders about the work of the church. When I was a coach, players would ask each other why so and so wasn't starting, but they wouldn't ask me, and I was the only one who knew the answer.

The third thing I know about asking is that—*the supply of good things available is almost boundless.* God's abundance is not in short supply. God said in Psalm 50:10, "Every animal of the forest is mine, and the cattle on a thousand hills." Whether it's happiness or virtue or even material blessings (should God so choose), they're not rationed. You'll never walk up to the window of life only to have the shade pulled and a sign put out that says, "Next window." God doesn't do that.

A prime example of the abundance of things that really matter was a young man from our church named Little Joe Greer. He had muscular dystrophy and was confined to a wheelchair, and he couldn't hold his head still. Yet he always had a warm smile and a spunky spirit. He always went to church, read his Bible every day, and was known for his sympathy. He'd give away anything he had to people in need. He made leather goods and sold them, and he also painted most of his life. He had to turn his paintings sideways and upside down to work on them since he couldn't get up and move around, but the results were beautiful.

Sadly, Little Joe's disease claimed his life. But in terms of an overflowing, happy, purposeful life, his had been fuller than most. Despite his handicaps, he lacked nothing that really counts. And his legacy is the many people he encouraged and helped and whose memories of him are full of love. Little Joe knew that life is like an ocean of good things.

John Rohn says that life is like the ocean. So, don't make the mistake of taking just a teaspoon to dip the ocean dry. You'll look funny, and kids will laugh at you. If you want to drain the ocean, you'd better take a bucket—a big one!

Fourth, *you usually get what you expect.* This matter of expectations is so important that an entire chapter is devoted to it (see Chapter 5). But for now, let me say again that this truth emphasizes the importance of fueling our minds with our dreams and goals for a better future. And be sure that what you want is what will really make you happy—in other words, that your priorities are in proper order.

The fifth truth I've learned is that *we need to ask persistently.* Again, this has been confirmed both biblically and in my experience. In Matthew 15:21-28, we have the story of a Canaanite woman who came to Jesus and asked Him to heal her daughter. When He first said no because she was not an Israelite, she persisted, showing great faith, and He eventually granted her request. In Luke 18:1-4, Jesus told a parable about how an unrighteous judge nonetheless granted justice to a widow because she persisted in pleading her case. Luke wrote that Jesus told the parable "to show them [His disciples] that they should always pray and not give up." Jesus told yet another story to make the same point back in Luke 11:5-13.

As the great preacher Charles Haddon Spurgeon once noted, "By perseverance the snail reached the ark." My friend Wimp Sanderson, whom I told about in the preceding chapter, probably felt just like that snail at times, but he eventually got to his goal, too.

Perseverance also usually pays off for me when I travel. If I fly somewhere and then need to rent a car at my destination, I'll have my travel agent reserve a car for me. But then when I arrive at the airport, I'll stop quickly at all the car rental counters and ask what their best rate is. Often I'll find that special, unadvertised rates are available that beat the deal my travel agent arranged. All it takes is a few minutes and some persistent asking. (If I don't find a better price, I can always fall back on the car my agent reserved.)

Sixth, I've learned *we need to ask the right way*. That means asking with humility and courtesy. It means *not* pouting or screaming or coming on like a two-ton truck. In other words, don't demand what you want. This also is such an important point that a whole chapter on it appears later in the book (see Chapter 6).

Why We Don't Ask

By now you should have a good idea of how we can get a lot of what we want just by asking. But if that's true—and it is—it raises this important question: Why do we so often fail to ask? The answer, of course, is fear. More specifically, I've found there are six kinds of fear that keep us from asking for what we want.

Number one and most obvious is *the fear of failure*. Oh, this one really gets us! Most of us have an absolute dread of failure. We interpret rejection of our requests as personal failure, and we'll go to great lengths to avoid that. So husbands and wives don't get what they want from each other because they're afraid to ask. Workers don't get what they want from their employers. Young men don't get dates. Salesmen don't close sales—they do everything right except ask for the order.

I'm convinced, and I often tell my students in class, "Hey, you've got to learn to fail in order to succeed." You've got to be good at losing if you want to win, because if you're

---

You usually get what you expect.

---

afraid to fail, you'll never try. And if you never try, you have no chance to succeed. It's that simple.

When Thomas Edison was being proclaimed a genius for inventing the electric light bulb, he explained that the secret of his success was his willingness to fail (and, of course, learn from his mistakes). The key to a reliable bulb had been finding the right filament material, and Edison said he tried 999 materials that didn't work before he discovered the one that did. In other words, only because he was willing to fail 999 times could he succeed the 1,000th time. That's the same openness to failure we all need.

Number two, closely related to the fear of failure, is *the fear of embarrassment*. Teachers often embarrass students at school, so students sit there and don't ask questions. I tell my students on the first day of class, "I'll never, never embarrass you. So relax and enjoy the class." And you can tell that some of them really relax; but others, by their posture or facial expressions, communicate, "Uh huh, I've heard that before, Jack." They don't believe you, so they test you.

Something happened to those students to cause them to be doubtful. Somewhere along about the second or third grade, perhaps, they asked a question in class, and everybody laughed. Then maybe a few months later, they asked another question, and this time the teacher said something that amounted to "Why don't you clean out your ears, Dummy?" That happened only a few times, and then those kids vowed to themselves, "That's it, I will never open my mouth in class again."

We need to develop the attitude that being embarrassed is not the end of the world. It's not even a big deal. Sooner or later, we have to decide that it's okay if we get embarrassed, as long as we're trying to learn and move toward our goals. We won't get what we want if we never ask.

Number three is *the fear of rejection*. This gets back to the way we equate rejection of a request with rejection of us personally. And there's nothing most of us crave more than to be loved and accepted by others. But the two are not the same. You can turn down my request without turning me down personally. We have to come to a point of believing that, hard as it may be.

Number four is *the fear of unworthiness—of not deserving what I want*. Most of us struggle with low self-esteem, so we tend to think we're not worthy of the best, either from people or from God. And in a theological sense that's true—we're sinners made part of God's family only by His grace. But we often scale back our requests or keep silent altogether because we feel undeserving.

We're kind of like the guy who had a flat tire out on a lonely country road. I don't even have a jack, he thought. What am I going to do? He walked along the road for a while, and then he saw a house way up on a hill. He figured they might have a jack, so he started up the hill. But as he walked he started to think, Even if they have a jack, will they let me borrow it? I doubt they'll want me to disturb them. He just kept talking to himself this way, working up his doubt and fear, until he got to the front door. And when the lady of the house opened the door, he blurted out, "You can just keep your old jack!"

But the fact is there's an ocean full of good things out there for us, and God loves us and He isn't stingy. Besides that, being God's adopted children gives us great worth. And the more I read about the lives of great people, the more I see that a big part of their greatness is that they had great goals, big dreams, that they pursued with determination. As they neared the end of their lives, I hear them saying, "I never asked for enough, never set my goals high enough. So much was available!"

Number five is *the fear of showing weakness.* "If I have to ask, I'll look weak or incapable," the mindset goes. And if there's anything we want to avoid, it's the appearance of weakness.

Men seem to have more of a problem with this than women—it's that old male ego. Men are the last to go to counselors, the last to ask for help, the last to read the instructions. A couple were driving in an unfamiliar area, looking for a place they'd never been to. "Honey, don't you think we'd better ask for directions?" the wife said.

"I can find it. Just give me another thirty minutes," the husband answered.

At the end of that time, when they still had no idea where they were, the wife said, "Honey, don't you think we're lost?"

"Yeah," he said, "but we're making great time!"

I learned how big a problem this fear is when I began using with my college students a little sheet titled "Thoughts That Cause Trouble." On it are forty statements, and I ask the students to mark the four or five they think are the most true—the ones that cause people the greatest trouble. I've had about two thousand students do this now, and certain answers come up often. Two of the most common are "I must never show my weakness" and "Strong people don't ask for help." This is what college students believe.

Now, where did they get those ideas? They picked them up somehow from their parents. But such attitudes are wrong for at least two reasons. First, it's the *wise* person who asks for help, not the weak person. When help is available and we need it and we refuse to ask for it, that's not strong but stupid. And second, such thinking is just plain un-Christian, because faith is based on admitting we're weak and sinful and in need of a Savior. Until we're willing to confess that need and throw ourselves on the Lord's mercy, we're lost in our sins.

On the other hand, when we're ready to admit our need of Jesus, we should also be able to admit our need in other areas. We're all needy—it's just a question of whether we'll admit that fact. "Confess your sins to each other," we're instructed in James 5:16.

One of the most moving speeches I ever heard was by a woman named Cynthia Rowland McClure. She held the audience spellbound as she told her life's story. Part of her story was a battle with bulimia and other eating disorders. Her life went downhill to the point that she ended up in a hospital. Then she said, "It was only when I was finally willing to admit I needed help—when I could say 'I need you. I need love. I need a hug'—that I started recovering."

Finally, number six is *the fear of begging,* which strikes at the heart of our pride. We're so afraid of losing our dignity, of having to swallow our pride. So we think in marriage, for example, Well, if I have to ask for it, she can just keep it. She ought to know what I want. Somehow we think our mates should be able to read our minds, or that if we have to ask for something that ruins our enjoyment of it. I don't know who sold us this worthless bill of goods, but that's just what it is.

Now, the truth is that asking does involve some swallowing of your pride, and that can hurt. But to get what you want, you have to ask, ask, ask. When I started coaching basketball, I knew nothing about the game, so every warm body I saw, I asked questions and took notes. When I became a college coach, I was still asking junior high coaches what they knew about the game and getting good tips. It's amazing what you can learn if you don't let pride get in the way. And I attribute whatever success I enjoyed as a coach to the fact that I never stopped asking questions.

A Request of Mr. Lincoln

During the Civil War, despite his busy schedule, Abraham Lincoln would occasionally take time to visit hospitals and cheer up the wounded soldiers. One time he came to the bed of a young soldier who was near death, and Lincoln said, "Is there anything I can do for you?"

The soldier, not realizing whom he was talking to, said, "Yes, there is. Would you please write a letter to my mother?"

So Lincoln sat down and wrote as the young man dictated. The letter read, "Dearest Mom, I was badly hurt while doing my duty, and I'll not recover. Don't sorrow too much for me. May God bless you and father. Please kiss Mary and John for me."

At that point the soldier grew so weak that he couldn't continue or even sign his name, so Lincoln finished the letter with this: "Written for your son at his request by Abraham Lincoln." And as he was put to put it in the envelope, the young man recovered enough to say, "May I see the letter? I'd like to read it once before you send it." When he got to the bottom and saw Lincoln's name, he was shocked. "Are you really the President?" he said.

Lincoln smiled and said simply, "Yes, I am. Is there anything more I can do for you?"

The soldier answered feebly, "Yes, Mr. President, would you mind holding my hand and seeing me through to the end?"

And so Abraham Lincoln, the President of the United States and certainly one of the greatest ever, took the soldier's hand and held it all through the night until finally, as the dawn began to break, the young man's grip weakened and he died.

As we go through life, and then as we draw near to those chilling waters of death, Jesus will be there beside us, and He'll say, "Is there anything I can do for you?" And if we'll just ask, we'll get the best He has to offer, including His hand on ours as we finally cross over to heaven.

Chapter Insights

1. Mr. Tate listed six truths he learned about asking. Summarize them briefly in your own words.
2. What are some things that keep you from asking for something you want?

3. What can you do to overcome that fear?
4. Read John 15:7. What does it mean to "remain in me"?
5. Are there any restrictions on this promise? If so, what are they?

CHAPTER 4

Get Excited

The simplest man, fired with enthusiasm, is more persuasive than the most eloquent without it.

— *Rochefoucauld*

A huge fire erupted in the downtown area of a large city, and firefighters responded from all over. The heat was so intense, however, that most of the fire trucks had to stop three and four blocks away from the blaze. Then, all of a sudden, one truck came screaming down the street in front of the burning buildings, its brakes screeching. It slammed against the curb, the firefighters scrambled out, and they began fighting the fire to save their lives.

The courage of this one company so inspired the other crews that when they saw it, they all raced forward and joined the battle. And before too long, the fire was out.

Shortly thereafter, the city fathers decided that fearless driver ought to be honored, so they invited him to City Hall for a ceremony. The mayor, the city council, and even his parents were there to praise his heroism and give him the keys to the city. As he was making the presentation, the mayor said to the firefighter, "Listen, if there's one thing you would want above everything else in the world, what is it?"

"A new set of brakes on that truck!" the man said.

Without realizing it, many of us have got the brakes on our lives today. We may have some ambitions that put one foot on the accelerator, but we've got the other foot jammed on the brake of our emotions and enthusiasm. And that's not a very efficient way to get where you're trying to go! Let yourself get excited! It's crucial to reaching your goals in life. If you can stay enthusiastic about what you're doing for thirty years—not just thirty minutes—the things you could accomplish are unbelievable.

Mike Wickett gives this illustration of real excitement: Imagine driving down the road, and all of a sudden you see something glittering beside a tree off to one side. You say to yourself, Hmm, I wonder what that is? I've got some time, so I think I'll go back and check it out. You go over and look, and sure enough, it's gold bullion! Not only that, but there's a sign saying "Finders, keepers." Wow! You can hardly contain yourself. You start loading the gold in your car, and soon the back end is almost on the ground and the tires are getting flattened. You've piled in as much as you can.

Figuring you've reached your limit, you start to walk away. But then you see a horde of gold even bigger than the first one! There must be a million dollars' worth there, but your car is already full. What are you going to do now? Of course! You'll call your best friend, Charlie!

Now, is this the way you call him: "Hello, Charlie. Is this a good time to call? I can call back later if you want"? Or would you call him up and say, "Charlie, listen to me! I don't care what you're doing, man, just get in your car and come down here right now!" Naturally, your call would be like the second example.

Well, I'm here to say that if you've chosen your goals carefully and they mean something to you, if you really want them, you should have the same kind of excitement about them as you'd have in calling Charlie. It'll make reaching them a lot easier and much more enjoyable.

My conviction on this point grew out of observations in two areas of life. First, as a basketball coach, I saw that teams that were excited and positive consistently played better than teams that were emotionally flat. In fact, teams with lesser talent often beat better teams purely because of greater excitement. I also noticed that if I was enthusiastic in practice, my team picked it up right away and rose to the same emotional level. It still happens today when I speak—the audience almost always mirrors my level of excitement.

Second, I've been around a lot of salesmen over the years, and I've seen how important enthusiasm is to their success. The ones who come across as genuinely excited about the products or services they're trying to sell are the ones who take home the big commission checks.

I also believe God encourages and rewards an enthusiastic approach to life. We read in Ecclesiastes 9:10, "Whatever your hand finds to do, *do it with all your might*" (emphasis added). God said through the prophet Jeremiah, "You will seek me and find me *when you seek me with all your heart*" (29:13, emphasis added).

In Luke 8 we see Jesus teaching in parables, and He told His disciples at one point that He used parables "so that [others], 'though seeing, . . . may not see; though hearing, . . . may not understand' " (v. 10). Theologians debate all Jesus meant by that, but I think one thing He meant was that He put the truth in hidden form so that those who want it would have to search for it. Wisdom doesn't come easily. No one's going to drive a truckload of it up to your house and dump it in your backyard for you. If you want it, you have to ask, and dig, dig, dig, and then you'll find it.

Make up your mind that nobody's going to hand you an exciting career, an exciting marriage, or an exciting life. If you want those things, you have to generate and maintain some enthusiasm yourself.

The Excitement Boomerang

One of the best things I've learned about enthusiasm is that it's like a boomerang—what you get excited about gets excited about you. This is especially good news since one of the reasons we often fail to act, to make positive changes in our lives, is the fear of what others will think. I've found that if you get excited, people respond by getting excited about you!

Now, I'll admit this may take a little time. When I first determined to be excited about life, one of the changes I made was to answer the superficial question "How are you today?" with something like "Great!" or "Fantastic!" At first, people looked at me kind of strange. But after a while, when I had made this a habit and people got used to it, I found that people were a lot brighter and more enthusiastic toward me when we met.

In the same way, the more I got excited about my marriage, the more my wife got excited about me. I made a point of showing more appreciation for her positive qualities and

---

Whatever you get excited about—gets excited about you.

---

accomplishments and saying less about her negatives, and she grew more positive about me. My speaking career also started to take off when I likewise got excited about it.

I also make an extra effort to be excited about and encourage my college students who aren't doing good work. They usually don't turn things around right away—they may still get an F. But they also often come back and repeat the class with a sense of excitement that was missing the first time.

You can't tell the difference, just by looking, between a magnetized and a nonmagnetized nail. But the people in the science department tell me that technically speaking, the difference is this: the magnetized nail has all its molecules running in the same direction, while the nonmagnetized nail has its molecules running in all different directions. In the same way, when you get some goals and they give focus to your life and you get excited about them, your life becomes a magnet. You start attracting the good things in life. That's what goals coupled with enthusiasm do for you—it's a powerful combination! You can do just about anything under the sun if you can get and stay excited about it. (See "Staying Excited" later in this chapter for more about the relationship of goals to enthusiasm.)

44

Life's Downward Pull

The reason we need to work hard to keep up our enthusiasm is that life exerts a downward pull on us. Life isn't naturally *for* us; neither is it neutral. Let me illustrate by comparing life to a garden plot where I want to grow some food.

Suppose that as soon as I buy the plot, I sit down in my rocker and say, "Bring me fruits and vegetables." Is that the way it works? Of course not. The plot isn't doing anything on its own to help me get ahead, and neither is life.

So suppose I clear off my plot and then till the ground, getting it ready for planting, but I haven't yet decided what I want to plant. Is it going to sit there and wait for me to decide? No, if I wait to plant my good seeds, the plot will soon be overrun with weeds. The plot isn't even neutral toward me—its natural tendency is to go downhill. And life's like that, too. It isn't neutral toward us but will take us downhill if we don't overcome it with enthusiasm.

Every virtue has to be defended, and every value has to be protected. If you let it, life will take everything you've got. It'll take your money and leave you not only poor but also in debt. It'll take away your attitude and give you stinking thinking. It'll take away your spirituality, too, the closeness of your walk with the Lord.

You might want to say, "Well, at least I should be able to relax once in a while." But what happens to the spawning salmon when he relaxes? He gets carried downstream in a hurry. A salmon has to keep humping it pretty hard just to stay even, and so do we.

I've seen this tendency for things to go downhill even in the routine of life. For example, when I was supposed to be learning spelling back in grade school, I chose to goof off instead. And I didn't just go downstream in that subject—the boat turned over, and I drowned! My spelling is a lot better today than it used to be, but it's been a slow process. When I started teaching, I was embarrassed to write on the blackboard because my spelling was so bad. (I learned to get around that by writing fast and illegibly!)

45

Another way to picture the situation is that life is like a tire with a high-pressure leak that can't be repaired. That leaves you with only two choices. You either keep it pumped up with enthusiasm, or else it goes flat. The bounce and the joy and excitement drain right out of living.

The Danger of Waiting

Last summer I had the privilege to speak in New England and Canada for a couple of weeks, and while in the area, I got to see that big "leak" they call Niagara. (One Texan, when he saw it, said: "Shoot, we've got a plumber in Texas who could fix that in fifteen minutes.") I also took the time to drive up the river, and you know what I noticed? When you get a few miles upstream, the river is cool, calm, and placid—nothing at all like the way it is at the falls.

I could imagine a guy in a little boat on the river three miles upstream from the falls; he has no idea what's waiting for him. People on the shore watch him go by; they could jump up and down, wave their hands, and yell at him, warning him to get out of the river before it's too late. But they assume the guy knows what he's doing.

If someone who understood the danger could get the guy's attention, there would be plenty of time for him to paddle over to the shore and safety. But if the guy waits until he's 100 yards from the falls to wake up and recognize his trouble, he's doomed. It won't do him any good to scream for help, and chances are that all the paddling in the world wouldn't save him. It's about over.

Today, your life may seem relatively calm and peaceful, so you may not see any urgency about choosing a purpose in life, setting some goals, and getting excited about them. But there are many standing on the shore, waving their arms and jumping up and down, warning you that if you wait too long, there'll come a point at which it's too late. Your life will be about over, and your choices will be about gone. My life has certainly been enriched by the materials of so many—Ron Willingham, Zig Ziglar, Jim Rohn, Bob Conklin, Denis Waitley, Charles Jones, Jim Newman, Ed

Forman, Dave Grant, to name a *few*—who have taught me to "stand on the shore and wave". This is why I *insist* that every person who has an automobile should have a cassette deck and good materials to feed their minds on and help them get excited about life. It's also a great way to get the most out of your driving and exercising time.

Ruts are dangerous things—graves with the ends knocked out. And the rut of a dull, unenthusiastic attitude toward life is no exception. As I wrote in my previous book *(Learning to Love)*, if we want to love better, we have to be prepared to change, and that requires us to take the painful step of breaking out of the comfort zones we've created for ourselves. There's no other way to make the kinds of improvements we want.

After one of my seminars in California a man told me his sad story. His wife had recently had an affair, and that woke them both up to how stale their relationship had grown. Now they saw the need to get excited about each other again, and they were trying to revive the marriage, but the well of care and enthusiasm had gone dry. There didn't seem to be anything left to pump. Besides, they were afraid that if they started making big changes now, people who had known them for thirty years would think they'd gone crazy.

Don't let something like that happen to you! Decide what's most important in your life, and get excited now, not when it seems too late.

Staying Excited

As important as enthusiasm is to getting what we want out of life, I know that staying enthusiastic day in and day out is a major challenge. It's so much easier, and natural, to slip back into a mundane approach to each day. So how do we stay enthusiastic? How do we maintain excitement about our goals and our pursuit of them?

First, it's a matter of staying focused on our goals. If we've chosen them with care and they're important to us, and if we keep them in the forefront of our minds using the steps outlined in Chapter 1, they build that fire of desire within us that powers us through each day.

This is why we should always have a set of goals we're working toward. As soon as we achieve one goal, we should replace it with another so we have that continuing source of motivation in our lives. Besides, even the goals we're still working on should be reviewed at least once a year, because our desires and priorities are always subject to change as time goes by. But certainly when one goal is reached, another should take its place.

In an interview with Olympic skating champion Brian Boitano since the conclusion of the Seoul games the reporter asked Boitano if he's happy now. Boitano thought for a bit, and then he answered, "Not as happy as I thought I'd be. It's a difficult time for me right now. There's a tremendous refocusing process going on. I worked all my years toward an Olympic medal. Now I have that. . . . I know that I have to move on. You have to put away the pictures."

Here's a young man (twenty-five years old at the time of this writing) who devoted the major part of his time and energy for many years to the achieving of one goal—winning an Olympic gold medal. He focused very hard on that goal, and his dream came true, but reaching it left him emotionally adrift. What does he work for now? What goal gives him the motivation to jump out of bed in the morning and tear into the day? Clearly, he needs to find some new goals, and soon, to put the spark back into his life.

There's something about the stretching and striving toward a goal, along with the excitement of anticipation, that's even more enjoyable than "getting to the top." That's why a guy who has worked himself up to millionaire status doesn't usually sit back and just live off the interest from his money. He enjoys the work, the setting and reaching of goals; looking forward to the rewards is more fulfilling than actually getting them.

Goals are simply one of the greatest sources of motivation I know.

The second major key to staying excited is staying close to God and His Word. Chapter 2 talks about seeing ourselves as working in partnership with God. When we have that perspective—working hand in glove with the Lord of the universe—how can we be anything *but* excited?

In 2 Corinthians 4, Paul talked about how he was "hard pressed on every side" (v. 8), but he could still say, "Though outwardly we are wasting away, yet inwardly we are being renewed day by day" (v. 16). And this was his renewing hope: "For our light and momentary troubles are achieving for us an eternal glory that far outweighs them all. So we fix our eyes not on what is seen, but on what is unseen" (vv. 17-18).

The prophet Isaiah wrote of this same renewing that comes from closeness to God and His eternal viewpoint: "Even youths grow tired and weary, and young men stumble and fall; but those who hope in the Lord will renew their strength. They will soar on wings like eagles, they will run and not grow weary, they will walk and not be faint" (Isa. 40:30-31).

A third key to staying excited is to keep close control on what you allow to fill your mind. The people you're around, the cassettes you listen to, the books and magazines you read, and the radio and television programs you take in— they all have a direct effect, either positive or negative, on

---

Nothing great was ever achieved without enthusiasm.

---

your thinking and your level of enthusiasm. *You will never rise above your level of thinking.* If you think bored and depressed and routine, that's what your life will be. If you want your life to be exciting and joyful, on the other hand, you have to keep yourself pumped up with exciting, motivating thoughts.

This is why I often listen to tapes and read books by such super people as Zig Ziglar, Ed Foreman, Jim Rohn, Gerald Jampolsky, Earl Nightingale, Denis Waitley and other inspiring people. They fuel my conviction that dreams can be made real and motivate me to pursue them all the harder.

I'm fortunate, also, to have friends like Wally Bullington, Jim Mankin, Karly Dodd, and Edsel Hughes who help me stay excited. They're excited, upbeat people themselves, which is a good start. They're also kind enough to make me feel special and capable, and they encourage me in the things I try to do, cheering me all the way. Our friends are a great influence so we should be careful to choose friends who are positive, encouraging, excited people if we want to be excited people.

Paul recognized the importance of what we fill our minds with in Philippians 4:8: "Finally, brothers, whatever is true . . . noble . . . right . . . pure . . . lovely . . . admirable—if anything is excellent or praiseworthy—think about such things." Dwelling on positive things like that is vital not only spiritually, but in all of life. We either make the effort to stay positive or we go flat on life.

A final key to staying excited is to focus on and build relationships and especially for young people, to build a good relationship with their parents. Simply put, there's not much peace and joy and excitement in life if you're not at peace with your parents.

Susan, one of my students, had rebelled against her parents and lost touch with them. As a result of that, I'm convinced, she disliked herself, saw herself as a loser, and so subconsciously set herself up to lose. Like many students I've seen who had a bad relationship with their parents, she often wouldn't get out of bed and get to class. To hear those students describe it, it's as if they'd start to get up, but the sheets would put all kinds of funny moves on them and pin them to the bed until they gave up the effort. When Susan didn't try to be clever with her excuses, she'd just claim to have been sick.

Not surprisingly, Susan did poor work in my class. And when she got back the bad grades on her papers and tests, she'd blame others for her failure—me, her parents, noisy students in the dorm when she was trying to study—whoever was convenient. Despite my best efforts to encourage her, her poor self-image wouldn't budge.

Later in the year, however, Susan reestablished a relationship with her parents. She went home emotionally as well as physically. Right away, her relationships with *everyone* improved, as did her performance in class. "Life seems to have a purpose it didn't have before," she said. "I want to do my best, and I want to win."

There's no substitute for good relationships with those closest to you, especially your family. That's why, Chapter 1 suggests that one of the major goals to begin to pursue right away should be in the area of family relationships.

So far we've considered the need to decide what you want, determine to pay the price, ask for it, and stay excited. But if you're like most people, even if you're trying to do all those things, you're probably thinking, *It sounds good but it won't really work for me.* And if that's what you're thinking, you're likely to be proved right. That's why we need to look next at the importance of your expectations.

Chapter Insights

1. Mr. Tate describes most people as having ambitions which press the accelerator and emotions and enthusiasm pressing the brake. Is that true? Why?
2. What are some of our allies in overcoming life's downward pull?
3. Why does God want us to be enthusiastic?
4. How can we stay excited?
5. What is your "excitement level"? What do you need to be excited about now? Why can't you get excited about it?

CHAPTER 5

Expect to Get It

---

*There is no medicine like hope,
no incentive so great, and no
tonic so powerful as expectation
of something tomorrow.*

— O. S. Marden

Words have great power, and those with the greatest effect are the ones we tell ourselves. For example, we tell ourselves how we're going to feel physically each day, and that's exactly how we feel. We can state it as a principle: *Whatever the mind harbors, the body manifests.* If a person stays up late one night, for instance, and has to get up early the next morning, his mental conversation usually goes something like this: "Boy, if I go to bed right now, I'll get only four hours' sleep. And I'm not even sleepy yet."

Then he goes to bed and tosses and turns all night because he knows he's going to be tired in the morning. He wants to sleep but knows he can't because he has to. So a half hour later his mind is saying, "Well, now I can only get three and a half hours of sleep, and I'm not asleep yet. Boy, am I going to be tired in the morning!"

He's expecting fatigue and has programmed it into his mind, and sure enough, he wakes up feeling incredibly tired. So as he's getting ready for work, he puts his eyes on "bag" and his body on "droop." And when he walks in the office door, he tells everybody, "Don't talk to me. I only had three hours' sleep."

Life can be very different. I have proven this by experience. And the key is what I tell myself to expect in situations like that. I might say something like "Hey, I'm only going to have about four hours' sleep tonight, but I'm going to feel good in the morning, because four hours are going to be sufficient for me. I'm going to wake up feeling refreshed. So body, sleep fast!" You may think I'm kidding, but I'm serious. I know that tired thoughts will give you tired feelings, while energetic thoughts will energize your whole mind and body.

One particular Friday night, I was up past midnight because my daughter was visiting. Right away, that violated one of my personal rules, which is to go to bed on the same day you get up. (I tell students that would solve about 90 percent of their problems.) Not only that, but I also had to get up at about 3:00 the next morning to drive over to Fort Worth and lead an all-day seminar. I spoke for eight hours, standing the whole time. (Psychologists say that requires more physical energy than digging a ditch for eight hours.)

After the seminar, I jumped in my car and drove the 150 miles back to Abilene so I could take my wife and daughter to a Ronnie Milsap concert that night. We got home around 10:00 or 10:30, and then I studied a little for my next day's duties, which included preaching twice and leading a Bible class.

How do I do those kinds of things? By programming myself positively. My wife tells me that my body handles stress better than most people, and that may be true. I know that your body's metabolism and your unique personality have much to do with your energy level. But I also know from experience that if you go to bed expecting to be tired the next day, you will be. If you go to bed expecting to feel great the next day however, you'll probably feel great. Whatever the mind harbors, the body manifests.

Expectations work the same way in something as mundane as finding a parking space. Most of my life, I went around looking for no place to park. Yes, you read it right. That sounds kind of dumb, but it's what I did. We'd be going to shop, and my wife would say, "Why don't you look for a space up front?"

"There's not going to be any place to park up there," I'd say as I drove to the front. I was literally going up there to look for no place to park. And sure enough, most every time, that's exactly what I found.

My wife, bless her heart, finally convinced me to apply my optimism to parking. So I started working on my expectations, and sometimes I even talk out loud to myself. "Okay now," I'll say, "whoever has my parking space, please move. I don't want to be stingy, and I don't mind your using it when I'm gone, but now I'm here, so kindly vacate my place." Then I imagine someone's backing out and apologizing to me! And you know what? I usually find a space near the front.

It may sound as if I'm off my rocker, but I'm telling you that expectations have a powerful effect. It happens more times than not.

There's an old saying that when you have a hammer in your hand, everything looks like a nail, and it's really true. In every situation, we're expecting something in particular to occur. And because we're looking for it, we generally find it. If you're holding that hammer, you're looking for things to use it on, so the world begins to appear full of nails.

We see an extreme example of this in Matthew 26:59-66, where Jesus' enemies were expecting to find something He had said or done for which they could condemn Him. They were so determined about it that they arranged for false witnesses to come in and lie against Him just to make sure. Anyone looking honestly and objectively at His life would have seen He was the sinless Son of God, but they weren't looking for the truth—only a reason to kill Him. And sure enough, eventually they found one they thought was good enough.

The Power of Choice

Throughout the years I spent in college, I carried a special notebook—it's in the museum now. And in the front of that notebook is a piece of frazzled, faded paper with a message on it that helped keep me in line during the tough times. I had to read it every time I opened the notebook. I don't even remember where I took the note, but it says, "It is not

54

the things that happen to us that make or break us. It is our mental reaction to those things that counts."

In other words, to make it, to keep pushing ahead when your progress is difficult or stalled, you have to stay positive. You have to keep expecting the best. We all experience pain, sorrow, defeats, and disappointments. And the difference between triumphing over them instead of being crushed by them is in how we choose to react.

Years ago, a young Englishman named Henry Fawcett went with his father on a hunting trip. And while they were hunting, the father's shotgun went off accidentally, permanently blinding Henry in both eyes. He was twenty years old at the time. Before the accident, he had been a bright, ambitious, young man with a great future. After the accident, no one would have been surprised if he had grown bitter and given up on life, and at first that's the way he felt.

One thing saved Henry, however. He loved his dad, and he knew his father was sick with grief over what he had done to his son. So for his father's sake, Henry chose to pretend that he was still interested in life, that he still hoped to be a useful citizen as an adult. In fact, he had no such hope.

Then the odd thing happened. Because he had to act positive and hopeful every day in his father's presence, a transformation gradually took place in Henry's mind. The pretense became reality, and it was as if by an act of the will, the spirit of despair was driven from him and a spirit of optimism remained. Henry went on to become a highly accomplished man. He was elected to the British Parliament, and then later he became England's postmaster general, from which office he made great improvements in the country's postal and telegraph systems. And it all happened because he chose, even deceptively at first, to keep hope alive.

The book of Proverbs, that great source of biblical wisdom, points repeatedly to the importance of how we react to things, especially words of correction or discipline. It paints the difference between choices in serious terms: "Anyone willing to be corrected is on the pathway to life. . . . The man who is often reproved but refuses to accept criticism will suddenly be broken and never have another chance. . . .

If you refuse criticism you will end in poverty and disgrace; if you accept criticism you are on the road to fame" (10:17; 29:1; 13:18, TLB).

How we choose to react to life and the things that happen in it makes all the difference.

The Power of Self-Talk

At the beginning of this chapter the power of words was stressed—especially the ones we say to ourselves. What we tell ourselves about ourselves and what's going to happen to us programs our expectations, and we usually get about what we expected. And that in turn raises the question, how do we change our self-talk so that we become positive in our expectations? Let me share how I began to change my own self-talk.

Before I decided to change, it seemed to me that nearly every day, I was teed off about something. It could be a driver who cut me off in traffic or a store clerk who

---

It is not the things that happen to us that make or break us.

---

shortchanged me or somebody who bruised my ego without intending to or even knowing he'd done it. But just one thing like that would keep me upset for the whole day.

As if that weren't bad enough, I was having one horrible, miserable, grumpy day after another. After seven days in a row like that, I ended up with a horrible, miserable, grumpy week. And after fifty-two such weeks in a row, you guessed it—I wound up with a horrible, miserable, grumpy year. Well, it finally dawned on me that if I kept this up, eventually I'd have a horrible, miserable, grumpy life, and I didn't want that. I was sick and tired of being "sick and tired."

The story is told of the old boy who died and was being carried to the grave when he sat up in the coffin and said, "Wait! Stop! Turn around! I forgot to be happy!" The last time I checked, though, they don't give you second chances after you're dead. It's a one-way trip. And I don't want to go to my grave with those regrets.

Now, I realized that big changes don't usually happen all at once, so I decided I'd try to have just one good day. Then I tried to have two good days. Next I went for three, but I messed up and had to start over. Still, I knew I was on the right track. And that's when I made myself a little promise that really changed my life forever.

I decided that a good place to start in turning around my self-talk was in the way I responded when people routinely asked me how I was doing. And I vowed that for thirty days, I would respond to the question with something positive and exciting, no matter how I felt. I didn't know exactly what effect it would have, and I didn't know what I would do at the end of the thirty days. But for that time I was going to be positive and see if it would help me to have some good days.

Why choose thirty days as the time frame? Because that's how long it takes us to get over the discomfort of doing something different and establish a new habit. If we can stick with something new for that long, it becomes ours.

The first day under this pledge stands clear in my memory. I was in the men's restroom at school at 8:00 in the morning when a guy walked in and said, "How're you doing?"

I said, "Oh, uh, oh, great! Doin' great!"

But right away he knew I wasn't, because when you have to think about it, you aren't. So he turned and faced me and challenged me on the spot: "Well, what's so great about it?"

"I just happened to look in the morning paper at the obituary column," I answered, "and I didn't find my name there, so I decided it was going to be a great day." And with that I walked out. (You have to learn to walk fast if you're going to do something like this. You're not trying to have a debate, so you don't hang around too long.)

Another time during my thirty days, I was walking to chapel when this professor walked up next to me, and I made a mistake and violated one of my principles. I said, "How are you doing?"

If you're trying to think positive and have a good day, you don't ever want to ask that question, because people will *tell* you. They'll whine and gripe and complain. "Did you see my stitches here?" "I've got the sniffles pretty bad today." And in Texas especially you'll get, "Well, the wind sure is blowing a lot today, ain't it?" (Since we can't control the wind or dust storms, even on those days when Lubbock seems to be blowing by, why can't we find something better to talk about?) It's like inviting people to dump garbage into your mind. (I don't mean we should lack compassion in the face of genuine need—I'm talking about those superficial greetings that fill our normal days.)

On this occasion, however, I asked the question, and he said, "Oh, pretty good." Then he asked politely, "How are you doing?"

"I'm doing great," I said.

Somewhat taken aback, he said, "Well, I suppose it's all relative."

But that's exactly my point. It's *not* all relative. Certain words fire the boiler on the engine of energy and motivation, and others pour water on the fire. Words are the most powerful fuel we have, and if you want to change the way you feel, you have to change the way you talk. What you verbalize, you emphasize. What you express, you impress. And what you emphasize, you multiply.

We all live in what Jim Newman calls the cycle of human behavior, which has three parts. We have first a belief system, those things we believe about ourselves and our world, our expectations, and so on. Second, out of those beliefs come our actions, our behavior. And we always act consistently with how we see ourselves. Our self-images and behavior may be wrong and even self-defeating, but they're always consistent. We couldn't live with ourselves otherwise.

On a simple level, for example, if you think of yourself as a 90 golfer and you get hot one day and shoot a 39 on the front nine, I can almost guarantee you won't match it on the back nine. You'll balloon to a 47 or 50 because of what your subconscious mind is telling your body, and afterward you'll say, "I knew that great scoring was too good to last!"

Then third, out of our actions comes our self-talk, what we tell ourselves about the world and ourselves and what we're doing. It's consistent with the other two items in the cycle, and it leads right back into our beliefs, usually reinforcing them, and the beat goes on. Once that cycle starts spinning in a certain direction, it seems to catch momentum and take off that way. And just as nothing succeeds like success, so also nothing fails like failure.

Now, of these three parts to the cycle, our self-talk is the easiest to change, so it's the best place to begin in becoming positive and learning to expect good things in life. And once we get the cycle spinning upward toward self-enhancement, it seems to get better and better—it multiplies.

This is not to say, however, that changing your self-talk is easy. It may be easier than trying to change the other two parts of the cycle, but it's still likely to be the hardest thing you've ever tried to do. If you're going to stick with a plan like the one I followed for thirty days, you've got to be about as tough as Hitler's mother-in-law, and that's pretty tough. Most people, you see, think they aren't having a very good day, and they want you to have a day about like theirs. They want to pull you down to where they are. When I started telling people I was doing great, I got all kinds of weird looks and double takes. It was as if they wanted to say, "What's wrong with you, Mr. Goody Two-Shoes? How come you think you're so special?"

If you stay with it, though, controlling the words you say out loud, gradually you'll see the words in your head begin to change. Your self-talk will grow more positive, and that change will multiply and in turn enhance your belief system and your actions. Words are that powerful, as the apostle James pointed out in chapter 3 of his book. The thirty-day program I described here revolutionized my self-talk, made me far more optimistic in my expectations that I had ever been before, and generally led to a host of improvements in my outlook on life and the quality of life I enjoyed.

Remember, too, that we're not alone in any good thing we try to do. As Paul said, "I can do everything through him who gives me strength," (Phil. 4:13). As we seek to serve

God, working in partnership with Him, He makes His resources available to us.

A Living Hope

This whole matter of expectations boils down to one word, hope. If we have hope, all things are possible, no matter what our circumstances. But if we've lost hope, they might as well start shoveling the dirt over us.

A man stopped to watch a Little League baseball game. "What's the score?" he called out to a boy.

The little guy answered, "We're behind eighteen to nothing."

"Wow!" the man said, "you're really getting beat."

"No, Sir," the boy said, "we haven't been to bat yet."

That's hope, and only with that kind of optimism would a comeback be possible. As a wise man once said, "Take from a man [or boy] his wealth, and you hinder him; take from him his purpose, and you slow him down. But take from man his hope, and you stop him. He can go on without wealth, and even without purpose, for a while. But he will not go on without hope" (C. Neil Strait).

Another illustration of the power of hope is the story of a man who lived a long time ago. He worked for the government for several years, and then he was told his services were no longer needed. With a few words, his hopes and expectations for the future were shattered. He felt rejected, humiliated, and defeated. By the time he got home that night, he was sunk in despair. He sat down and wouldn't—couldn't—tell his wife anything. He was too embarrassed. When she asked what was wrong, he just shook his head.

Finally, later that evening, the man was able to tell his wife what had happened. He poured out all the pain and hopelessness he felt. Her response was to go into another room and get a pen, ink, and paper, and then come back and put them in front of him. She put her arms around his shoulders and said, "Honey, now you will be able to write your book."

"My book?" he said.

"Yes, Dear, your book—the one you've always wanted to write but didn't have the time to."

After a few minutes, with that flicker of hope lighting a candle in the darkness of his despair, the man picked up the pen and began to write—slowly at first, even hesitantly. But then his thoughts began to flow, his pen began to move, and he really got into the groove. Thus was born, over 100 years ago, one of the great novels in American literature, Nathaniel Hawthorne's *The Scarlet Letter*. It grew out of the lowest point in his life, and it grew out of hope.

The lack of hope is a killer. A young American Marine had survived two years in a Viet Cong prison camp in relatively good health during the Vietnam War. This was in large part because the camp commander had promised to release him if he cooperated. Since the Marine had seen this happen with other prisoners, he was hopeful, and he became a model POW and the leader of the camp's "thought reform" group.

As time went by, however, the Marine gradually came to realize his captor had lied to him. When the full realization of this hit and his hope evaporated, the young man became a zombie. He refused to do any work, rejected all offers of food and encouragement, and simply lay on his cot, sucking his thumb. Within a few weeks, he was dead.

Fortunately, *we who belong to Christ need never be without hope*, for the Father calls us to a living, imperishable hope. We read in 1 Peter 1:3-5, "Praise be to the God and Father of our Lord Jesus Christ! In his great mercy he has given us new birth into a living hope through the resurrection of Jesus Christ from the dead, and into an inheritance that can never perish, spoil or fade—kept in heaven for you, who through faith are shielded by God's power."

This hope, Peter wrote out of his experience and the inspiration of the Holy Spirit, can sustain us even in the most difficult circumstances: "In this [hope] you greatly rejoice, though now for a little while you may have had to suffer grief in all kinds of trials. These have come so that your faith—of greater worth than gold, which perishes even though refined by fire—may be proved genuine and may result in praise, glory and honor when Jesus Christ is revealed. Though you have not seen him, you love him . . . and are filled with an inexpressible and glorious joy" (1 Pe. 1:6-8).

Our hope is further fueled by these words of Jesus, spoken after He ordered His followers to go and make disciples: "Surely I am with you always, to the very end of the age" (Mt. 28:20). Reciting Psalm 23 is another great hope booster. And if that's not enough, we have the ringing, hope-filled assurance of Romans 8:38: "I am convinced that neither death

---

We who belong to Christ need never be without hope.

---

nor life, nor angels nor demons, neither the present nor the future, nor any powers, neither height nor depth, nor anything else in all creation, will be able to separate us from the love of God that is in Christ Jesus our Lord." That about covers it, folks! Nothing can take away our hope in Christ.

Anchored to such a hope, we can look expectantly and optimistically toward the future. We can share the outlook of the great architect Frank Lloyd Wright who, when asked at age eighty-three which of his works he considered his masterpiece, said, "My next one." We, too, can anticipate that tomorrow will be a better day, that our next piece of work will be our best ever, and that every day we'll grow closer to those we love.

A lot of hard work is involved in making those dreams come true, but it all begins with *expecting* to get what we want out of life.

Chapter Insights

1. Mr. Tate says self-talk is vital to a positive outlook. Reflect on your own self-talk, is it positive or negative?

2. What do you expect from life? Think about an upcoming opportunity or problem. How do you feel about the outcome?
3. What does Mr. Tate mean when he refers to "living hope?"
4. Read Luke 11:11-13. What should we expect from God?
5. Should we expect life to always be smooth sailing? Why?

CHAPTER 6

Don't Demand

The Christian understanding of power is that it is found most often in weakness.

— *Charles Colson*

When Bobbie and I first moved from Alabama to Texas, it took us a while to get straightened out concerning the laws on changing car tags. At that time, Alabama was not requiring inspection stickers, so we were not aware that one might be necessary in Texas. One Sunday, after we had put Texas plates on the car (but no inspection sticker), we were stopped on the way home from church by a policeman. This officer insisted not only that we were liable for a fine, but also that I couldn't *drive* the car anymore until I had the sticker. (He refused to take our ignorance into consideration!)

"How am I going to get it inspected if I can't drive it?" I said angrily.

We really got into a battle over it—I, insisting he see it my way and make an allowance for me—he, insisting I was going to get a fine and drive the car no more until it displayed an inspection sticker. I got more upset than I've ever been, with just a few exceptions. But you can guess whose opinion won out, and it wasn't only because he was wearing the badge—I wasn't exactly reading from *How to Win Friends and Influence People,* either. I've tried to learn from that experience, and I use that as an illustration of how demanding does not work.

When the shoe has been on the other foot and people have demanded things of me, I've understood how that policeman must have felt. Has your back ever kind of bowed up when someone demanded something of you and you determined you weren't going to give them what they wanted if you could help it? That's a bad attitude, but it's human nature, and it's why we seldom get what we want by demanding, unless we have some kind of power over the other person. So in this chapter I want to emphasize the point that while we should ask for what we want (see Chapter 3) and expect to get it (see Chapter 5), the *way* we ask is crucial to our getting it.

Why We Do It

It's my observation that, unfortunately, demanding is the normal way of asking. Whether it's a child requesting something of his parents, a husband asking his wife for something, or a nation negotiating with another country, it seems natural to demand. Why? Because we're fearful concerning our rights, privileges, places, and prestige. In other words, our egos are involved. And we're afraid that unless we demand, the other person is going to run over us, mistreat us, deny us our rights and privileges, or bruise our precious egos.

Ego can make you do incredibly dumb things. Once in a fast-food restaurant with my wife, daughter, and a niece, when I picked up our food I noticed there were no french fries on the tray. Since I knew I had ordered some, I said, "I ordered french fries."

"Okay," the young man behind the counter said, and he gave me some fries. I thought that made the order correct.

When I got the food to the table, however, one of the girls said, "I ordered french fries, too."

"Okay," I said, and I went back up to the front, where I told the young man, "I actually ordered two fries. Will you give me another?"

"Well, bring your receipt up here," he said.

Now, that was a reasonable request, but immediately my ego said, "Wait a minute! You don't know me—I'm an honest guy. You can't treat me like this!" And what I actually said was, "I'm not bringing the ticket up here. I trusted you, you can trust me. If you don't believe me, I'll *pay* for another order of fries." That was silly of me, yet it's so typical of human nature. (He gave me the fries, then I went back to the table and *checked the ticket!*)

Another reason we tend to demand is that we quickly turn privileges into rights and needs. There's a big difference between privileges and rights, but most of the time we conveniently mix them up. A privilege is something that's given to us and that can rightfully be taken away by the giver under the proper circumstances. A right, on the other hand, is something to which we're entitled, something that should never be taken away except under the most extreme circumstances, and something worth fighting and even dying for.

Borrowing my neighbor's lawn mower, for example, is a privilege he gives me, and he can require its return any time he wants. Our freedom, on the other hand, is a God-given right that can be taken away only under the most serious circumstances (like being fairly tried and convicted of a crime), and many people have died over the years to preserve our freedoms.

But the distinction between privilege and right gets easily blurred. If I keep my neighbor's lawn mower for a while, I'm likely to start thinking of it as at least partly mine, and then I'll be resentful when he comes and asks for it back. I'm likely to think, *Yeah, you can use it, but hurry up and return it!*

Bill Gothard, in his seminars, suggests an exercise that helps us to distinguish between rights and privileges. Imagine that one day you see someone walk up to your mailbox and put something in it. Curious, you go out and see what it is, and lo and behold, it's a crisp, new $1,000 bill! Wow! you think. This is my lucky day! I can't believe this is happening! Then you call all your friends and tell them about your incredibly good fortune.

Next day, at the same time, you just happen to be looking out your front window, and here comes this same guy walking up to your house again. You wonder, Could it be? Do you reckon? He leaves something in your mailbox, you go dashing out, and sure enough, there's another new $1,000 bill. You get excited all over again. And much to your amazement and delight, this continues every day like clockwork for about three weeks.

How would you be feeling by the end of that time? The same as you did the first day? Well, suppose that on the twenty-second day, you see this guy walking down the sidewalk toward your house at the regular hour—only this time he walks right past your place and turns in at your

---

Don't confuse privileges with rights.

---

next-door neighbor's house. You watch as he goes up to the mailbox and puts something inside. "Wait a minute!" you shout. "You're putting *my* money in his mailbox!"

You had no right to any of that money, did you? It was a privilege—oh, what a privilege! But after you received the privilege for a while, you began to think you were entitled to it. So what was he doing giving your money to someone else? You had made it into a right. Now, this example is a little far-fetched, but we do the same kind of thing every day, and when we do, we're quick to demand what we think of as rightfully ours.

No Way to Be Happy

When we lived in Alabama, I had a confrontation with a man we'll call Glenn. In the church where we were members, he was saying some things about the work and my role in it that weren't true. I got caught up in the situation and I had a bad attitude. For one thing, I got angry. And for another I was determined to prove my rightness in the matter. In fact, I was far more concerned about being proved right than I was about making peace with Glenn or restoring peace in the church as a whole.

Through my angry demand that some truths be presented, I got my way. Glenn was forced to admit he was wrong, and my rightness was confirmed. This is one of the few times I can remember when demanding something got me what I wanted. But you know what? After I got my way, I really wasn't happy. I didn't enjoy the victory at all—I actually felt worse than I had before.

The hollowness of my conquest, I soon realized, stemmed from the way I had gone about it. The anger, self-righteousness, wounded ego, and lack of love I had displayed weren't anything to be happy about. My means of winning were no better than Glenn's falsehoods that had started the whole conflict.

That's how I learned an important lesson. *When you demand what you want, you're not going to be happy, even if you get it.* Only after I apologized to Glenn for the way I had conducted myself did I feel any peace and happiness over how the matter had turned out.

There are at least two reasons why you don't really win by demanding—even if it gets you what you wanted. First, you'll never get the best people have to offer. Instead, you'll get the leftovers, the crumbs, and those only grudgingly. Nobody who's forced to cooperate is going to do any more than the bare necessity, and you'll sense that's exactly what you're getting. You don't make any friends, either—I certainly didn't make an ally out of Glenn by the way I drove him into "submission."

Second, when you get your way by demanding, you never feel good about yourself. You lose honor, joy, and feelings of love. You really cheat yourself. It's kind of like losing a dollar to gain a quarter. Can you picture a guy giving up his greenback and saying, "Hey, but I got a quarter!" That wouldn't be very smart, yet it's just the way most of us live.

Take it from someone who's learned in the school of hard knocks—demanding is no way to be happy, even when it "works."

The Futility of Trying to Control

A big part of demanding our own way in daily life is the struggle to control other people, to manipulate them into meeting our needs in the way we prefer. It's a doomed cause. Think of how difficult it is to control just one person—your spouse or a child, for example. As futile as that is, you should know you're never going to control the whole world so as to get your own way all the time.

The fact is that even when your needs are legitimate, people will disappoint and hurt you. They usually don't have your standards, so they don't do what you think they should. Trying to control them is a sure route to unhappiness.

A few years ago, a sad TV movie that had a happy ending (ironically) brought this negative point home to me. It was called "Who Will Love My Children?," and it was about a woman who was dying of cancer, whose husband was alcoholic, and who worried about what would become of her nine children when she died. She got all of them placed in adoptive homes except for one small boy who had "spells" and so wasn't quite as appealing to potential parents as the others. She ended up having to leave him in an orphanage, which broke both their hearts.

In the next scene, the children and their adoptive families were walking away from the closed grave. The couple who adopted the next-oldest boy were talking, knowing the little boy was stuck in the orphanage, and the husband said, "Look, if we had kids of our own, there's no guarantee they would be well or whole either."

So they went to visit the boy, and the older brother said, "We're gonna move to California."

"I know," the little boy said. "I can't go, because I have spells." It was a real tear-jerker.

In the film's final scene, however, we saw the car pull up in front of the orphanage. The husband went inside and came back out holding the little boy's hand. The older brother jumped out of the car, ran to grab his brother, and they rolled and wrestled playfully in the grass. "I told ya they was gonna get ya," he said. And then the family got in the car and drove away.

That's when the irony hit me. As sweet as the story was, there's no *guarantee* of that kind of love in this world. Many orphans get left behind. The fact is that some people will love you and some won't. Some will accept you, and some will reject you. You just can't *depend* on people every time, even when you have real needs. So trying to control them is a futile way to try to be happy. A better way is to realize that we *can* depend on God and His love.

Antidotes to Demanding

If demanding either doesn't work or doesn't make us happy when it does work, what's the alternative? How do we learn a better way of getting along and getting what we want out of life? There are three approaches that work for me.

The first is what I call *turning frustrations into fascinations.* As prone as we are to be demanding under ordinary circumstances, we get even more demanding when we grow frustrated and (usually) angry. And in those situations, I'm learning to turn frustration into something good by concentrating on something interesting which I can focus my attention on to get my mind off the difficulty. Let me illustrate just what I mean.

One time I drove home and parked the car in the driveway. Then, without thinking, I locked the doors and got out, leaving the keys in the ignition. As soon as I closed the car door, I realized what I had done and that there was no way to get into the house—or back into the car. I also knew Bobbie was gone and she wouldn't be home for several hours. What was I to do?

In the past, I would have grown frustrated immediately and gotten angrier and angrier as the minutes went by. I would have sat waiting on the front porch, stewing in my dejection, telling myself how stupid I was. Instead, however, I turned my frustration into fascination. I noticed some honey bees working away on a flowering tree in the yard, and I walked over to watch. As they worked their way in and out, gathering the nectar, I became absorbed. I really enjoyed watching them. And before I knew it, a neighbor friend came home, I was able to call Bobbie, and she drove back and let me into the car so I could get my keys.

I think you'll agree that was a much healthier approach than letting my frustration build up and then taking it out on Bobbie when she got back.

Another time, I was driving through Shreveport, Louisiana, when I got stuck in some awful stop-and-go traffic. Because of an accident in which a tanker truck spilled sulfuric acid, we were routed off the interstate and had to drive on city streets right through the middle of downtown. We were barely moving, and I could see my schedule for getting where I was going flying right out the car window.

Again, in the past this would have given me a major case of frustration and anger. But this time I chose to turn the frustration into fascination. I noticed there were a lot of old buildings downtown with beautiful architectural details. They were the kind of buildings that just aren't built anymore, either because the necessary skills have died out or because it would be too expensive. As we poked along, I looked those buildings over closely, admiring their beauty and the quality of workmanship. I still remember them clearly. Before long, it seemed, we were out of the heavy traffic and rolling down the highway again. We would not have moved any faster if I had become angry and frustrated, and I certainly enjoyed the time spent in slow-moving traffic better.

A second approach is to *change our self-talk regarding needs and preferences.* Because of the powerful effect our words have on us, as already mentioned, we really handicap ourselves emotionally when we go around saying "I *need* this" and "I *need* that." Our actual needs are really quite simple. We need air, some food and water, some shelter and clothing and love—and that's about it. Everything beyond that is desire and preference. As soon as we turn our preferences into needs, happiness walks out the front door.

Paul wrote to Timothy, "We brought nothing into the world, and we can take nothing out of it. But if we have food and clothing, we will be content with that" (1 Ti. 6:7-8). That's the ideal attitude we should aim for, simply having our basic needs met. But we're tempted to say, "Paul, didn't you know that people in the late twentieth century in America would be reading this? Who are you kidding?"

We say "I really need a new dress" or "I've got to get a new car" or "I need that promotion so I can get the raise that goes with it." But a need is something you've got to have, something your doing without will cause pain. The truth is usually that you'd *like* a new dress, a new car would boost your ego, and you *want* the promotion so you can achieve the level of lifestyle you've been dreaming about. (There's nothing wrong with having and pursuing dreams, but let's be *honest* about what they are.)

When we tell ourselves repeatedly that we need a certain something—a new car, let's say—our emotions get wrapped up in it, and before long it become a psychological addiction. Then the feeling grows that we've got to have it. According to Ken Keyes, Jr. the definition of a psychological addiction is "something conditioned into the mind that, if not satisfied, automatically triggers a negative emotion such as anger, fear, jealousy, anxiety, sorrow, or resentment."

The unhappiness that results from unsatisfied addictions is like a disease. It saps energy and life. It keeps you from being interested in the many good and worthwhile things

---

Turn your frustrations into fascinations.

---

that are going on around you, not to mention the people who make up your life. And that, in turn, harms your Christian witness. If there's no joy in your life, what appeal is there to a nonbeliever?

I'm convinced that much of our suffering and unhappiness grows out of our demands and addictions. I know hearing that for the first time doesn't solve all the problems, but think about it. Recall your own experiences and see if much of the time your past unhappiness wasn't caused by your demands and addictions.

This is why it's good to start talking to ourselves in terms of preferences instead of needs. It's kind of like a joke we'd sometimes play when I was growing up and we were choosing sides for a ballgame. Some smart aleck would say,

"Let's flip a coin to see who picks first. Heads I win, tails you lose." I *try* to say that to myself about most things in life. If I get what I want, that's great. I love it and enjoy it. But if I don't get it, I'm not unhappy, either, because it was just a preference. I've already got everything I really need. So either way it goes, I win. Isn't that beautiful?

If you want to develop this attitude, look at the things you're telling yourself these days. Ask yourself about each of them, "Is this something I really need, or is it a preference?" And if it's a preference, start catching yourself each time you describe it (to yourself or someone else) as a need, and change your language to describe it accurately.

It's a good idea, too, to make a list of all the things you have to be thankful for, then carry the list around with you and review it every once in a while. Make a special point of looking it over whenever you start to feel down about some unfulfilled desire.

Jesus' Example

Finally, the most important approach to overcoming the tendency to demand is to *adopt the submissive attitude modeled by Jesus Christ*. When facing the horror of the cross, He said to the Father, "Not my will but thine be done." In John 4:34 He said, "My food . . . is to do the will of him who sent me and to finish his work." And Jesus' response to enemies? "When they hurled their insults at him, he did not retaliate; when he suffered, he made no threats" (1 Pe. 2:23). Then Jesus said, "If anyone would come after me, he must deny himself and take up his cross daily and follow me" (Lk. 9:23).

This is why we read commands like these in the Bible: "Honor one another above yourselves" (Ro. 12:10); "Submit to one another out of reverence for Christ" (Eph. 5:21); "Do nothing out of selfish ambition or vain conceit, but in humility consider others better than yourselves. Each of you should look not only to your own interests, but also to the interests of others. Your attitude should be the same as that of Christ Jesus" (Phil. 2:3-5). That's about as far as we can get from a demanding attitude, isn't it?

73

The story isn't finished yet, however. Following Jesus isn't just a matter of self-denial for the sake of self-denial. Jesus also said, "Whoever loses his life for me and for the gospel will save it" (Mk. 8:35). He added, "Blessed are the meek, for they will inherit the earth" (Mt. 5:5). And the psalmist said, "He [God] guides the humble in what is right and teaches them his way" (Ps. 25:9). The prophet Isaiah said, "The meek also shall increase *their* joy in the Lord" (Is. 29:19, KJV).

In other words, a life of submissiveness is the way you get the most that's gettable and enjoy what you're getting. Demanding what you want isn't the way.

There's a quiet power in living a Christlike life. The French emperor Napoleon observed that he, Alexander the Great, Caesar, and Charlemagne had all founded empires based on force. Jesus, however, founded His kingdom on love and humility. Today there are millions who have committed their lives to Jesus and would probably die for Him. How many would die for Napoleon or Caesar? So which is the greater power?

Christ's life is the way to greater happiness. Helen Keller, blind all her life, was nonetheless typical of Jesus' followers when she said in her later years, "Life is so beautiful." Napoleon, on the other hand, after conquering all of Europe, said, "I've never known five happy days in my life."

When I was the basketball coach at ACU, I felt firsthand the power and happiness of a submissive lifestyle. On taking the job, I had hired a full-time assistant coach; but he left after a while, as is common in the profession. And when he left, the "powers that be" said they didn't think I needed another full-time assistant to replace him. With my many responsibilities in trying to win a conference championship, recruiting, and all the rest, being without a full-time assistant was like having an arm or a leg cut off. But even though I made every argument I could, they wouldn't change their minds.

As frustrated as I was, I chose to be submissive. I remember telling myself over and over that as long as I worked for the school, I was going to work for them until it got to where I felt I couldn't work for them, and then I'd leave.

But in the meantime, I wasn't going to talk about how I was being mistreated and didn't have a chance to win. I was going to do the best job I could under the circumstances and stay patient.

Eventually I was able to hire another full-time assistant, and I think it happened faster than it otherwise might have because I was submissive and not demanding. I was also happier the whole time than I would have been if I'd fueled my frustration, and I remained friends with people I could have easily alienated. So the way I see it, I won in all respects because I was submissive.

How could Jesus live the life He did, and how can we follow? First, Jesus knew who He was, so He didn't waste time and effort trying to prove to somebody who He was, the way we often do. John 13:3 says, "Jesus knew that the Father had put all things under his power, and that he had come from God and was returning to God." He knew where He had come from and where He was going—He knew exactly who He was.

That verse also suggests the second reason Jesus could live as He did: He knew His purpose. He had come from God to do a specific work, the work of salvation and the setting of an example, and when it was done He was going home. And while He was here, that purpose kept His life focused. That's why He could say as He died, "It is finished" (John 19:30).

Third, Jesus could live such a life because He had a different standard. He didn't buy into the world's standards about how to live or what to live for. If there's any one message that comes through loud and clear in Jesus' great Sermon on the Mount, it's "Be different. My standards are not the world's." Paul repeated this theme often, perhaps most memorably in Romans 12:2, where he wrote, "Do not conform any longer to the pattern of this world, but be transformed by the renewing of your mind."

In the same way, if we understand who we are—children of God who will one day go to spend eternity with Him— what our great purpose is—to take as many others as possible with us to heaven—and that we have different standards—

the words and example of our Savior—we'll be ready to live as He lived and we will overflow with joy.

Chapter Insights

1. How is submissiveness a way to get the best and enjoy what you've got?
2. Think of a time when you demanded something and got your way. How did you feel? How do you think the other person felt?
3. Read James 4:2-3. What do those verses say about why we don't always get what we ask of God?
4. Is it ever right to make demands of God? Of other people? Why?
5. What are some antidotes to demanding?

CHAPTER 7

Accept What Is—Stop Resisting Reality

You can't have rosy thoughts about the future when your mind is full of blues about the past.

— *Anonymous*

The story is told of two cowboys and an Indian who rode hard together all day long. Toward evening, the cowboys started talking about how hungry they were and the big meal they planned to devour when they got to town. Then they asked the Indian if he was hungry. He shook his head and said "No."

Finally, they arrived at their destination, stabled their horses, and dashed into the restaurant. All three ordered steaks with all the trimmings, and when their dinners arrived, the Indian wolfed his down faster than either of the cowboys. He gobbled everything in sight.

Watching him with some amusement, one of his friends reminded him that less than an hour before, he had said he wasn't hungry. So why was he shoveling it in now?

"Not wise to be hungry then," the Indian said. "No food."

That Indian knew something we all need. He had learned to be content with what he had at the moment, to not let thoughts of what he didn't have or how he might be better off ruin his attitude. He could make the most of the present and not long for full stomachs in the past or anguish over hopes of future feasts. In short, he accepted reality for what it was and was much the happier for it.

Perhaps without even knowing it, he echoed the thoughts of the apostle Paul: "I have learned to be content whatever the circumstances. I know what it is to be in need, and I know what it is to have plenty. I have learned the secret of being content in any and every situation, whether well fed or hungry" (Php. 4:11-12).

The fact is that life will never be perfect or problem-free. Everyone has troubles. The history of the human race can be summed up in one phrase: opportunity mixed with difficulty. That's the way it's always been, that's the way it is now, and that's the way it will always be until Jesus returns. Furthermore, not even the richest people in the world can buy everything they might want, because there just isn't enough money, and most worthwhile things aren't for sale anyway.

Sooner or later, then, if we want to be happy, we have to choose to be content in a very imperfect world.

In the first half of this book, we looked at how to get what you want, the most that's gettable. But there's a second side to the story that we need to consider now, because getting what you want is only half of what it takes to be truly happy and satisfied in this life. The other half is learning to want whatever it is you have. And that begins with accepting reality as it is at the moment.

Happiness in the Routine

Much of life consists of routines—getting up at the same time every day, getting yourself ready, helping the kids get ready, driving the same way to work, doing the same job, driving home the same way, doing the same things at night as always. It's easy to feel you're in a rut, to look at someone else's life or career and think that would be a lot more interesting than your own. The feeling is so common that we've got a cliché to picture it: "The grass is always greener on the other side of the fence."

A new job or lifestyle is no guarantee of happiness. Surveys show that a person who quits a job he doesn't like is probably going to be unhappy in his new job, too. The problem usually isn't with the job itself, you see, but with the person's attitude. And the fact is that however exciting a job or lifestyle looks from a distance, every job, every company, and every lifestyle has its problems and shortcomings. It's a lot easier to get excited about your present position than it is to find the perfect one.

Some people look at my life, which includes teaching, traveling, speaking, and writing, and think it must be pretty exciting. But believe me, what I do becomes awfully routine, too. I pack my books and clothes, drive to the airport, eat those peanuts and drink those Cokes on the plane, land somewhere and rent a car, drive to a hotel, do my seminar, and then do it all in reverse. Sometimes I don't know what day it is or what town I'm in.

It's also not uncommon for me to arrive home in the wee hours of the morning, get just a few hours' sleep, and then get up and teach an early class. If you think that's glamorous, try it just a time or two.

The fact is that if you can't get excited about what you do *now*—you probably would not get excited doing something else. So if you want happiness, you need to find it in the routines—the everyday, ordinary "stuff" of your life. You need to find joy in cooking this meal, washing these dishes, balancing that checkbook, reading this book to your child, taking tonight's walk with your spouse. Get excited about the life you have now, and it will begin to get excited about you.

Why Do We Struggle?

Why is it such a struggle to accept reality? Why do we want to either demand instant solutions to our problems or try to run away from them? There are three major reasons common to us all.

First, we tend to believe that if we accept things as they are, even if only for the moment, we'll be stuck with what we have now, and life will never get any better. It's as if we equate accepting reality with giving up on the future.

Nothing could be further from the truth, however. The first half of this book explains how you can get the things you really want in life. You can make your life into just about whatever you want it to be. Choosing to accept things as they are for now actually gives you a power to improve your life that you don't get by complaining or running. More will be said about this later in the chapter.

Second, we rob ourselves of enjoyment in the present by dwelling on the past or daydreaming about the future. How many people do you know who live in bygone days, constantly recalling some time when their hazy memories tell them life was much sweeter, more loving, more fulfilling,

---

Happiness is the journey, not the destination.

---

or whatever? I'll bet you could name several. When our focus is on an idealized past, there's no way we can appreciate the good things in the present and enjoy the lives we're living now.

While living in the past is especially common among the elderly, we're all prone to make the mistake of comparing the present to our daydreams for the future and finding the present lacking. We picture in our minds some thing or some career or some relationship we'd like to have and then spend our time pining for it. "If only I could make another $10,000 a year!" "If only I could have a romance like Romeo and Juliet!" "If only my kids were through school so I could have some time to myself!"

I read recently that the average American believes that if could make $27.50 more per week, he'd be happy. But you know what? If we got that $27.50 extra per week, we'd soon conclude we needed *another* $27.50 per week to *really* be happy. The problem with our lack of happiness isn't how much we have or don't have, but our attitude toward it.

A book published a few years ago was called *Getting By on $100,000 a Year.* At first glance, that sounds kind of silly. I don't know about you, but somehow I think I could manage on such an income. The fact is, however, that many people making that kind of money struggle to make ends meet just as much as you and I do on much lesser incomes. (They may enjoy a higher standard of living, but they still struggle to pay all their bills.) Why? Because outgo expands to match (or even exceed) income—I think it's a corollary of Murphy's Law. Because like the rest of us, the wealthy tend to think happiness lies in getting just a few more things than they already have.

The danger of dwelling on the future can be seen clearly in sports. Many times in my college coaching career, I saw a superior team lose to an inferior one because the better squad was "looking ahead" to what was supposed to be a tougher game. Because the players took the present opponent too lightly, they didn't concentrate on doing their best in the game at hand, and they went down to defeat. And in a similar way, many people suffer loss day after day.

Think back ten years in your life. What did you tell yourself then would make you happy? What did you think you needed in order to be satisfied that you didn't already have? Now let me ask. Do you have most or all of those things today? Chances are you do. And are you happier as a result? Probably not. It all depends on your attitude, doesn't it?

Ten years ago, when I was dreaming of being a professional speaker with a full schedule of engagements, I dreamed of making enough so my wife wouldn't have to work outside the home. For the last few years, that's been true.

Does that mean I'm happier now than I was ten years ago? Not necessarily. The fact is that I *am* happier now, but it's because my attitude is improving—not because of the additional income. I'm learning to live in what Spencer Johnson calls "the precious present." (You notice I put this in the *progressive* tense!)

An elderly lady known for her joyful spirit was asked the secret of her happiness. She replied, "I make the most of what comes and the least of what goes." What a great attitude! She made the most of the present, enjoying the moment and not worrying about what she used to have or didn't yet have.

Songwriter Johnny Mercer put it like this: "Accentuate the positive, eliminate the negative." Make the most of every blessing, opportunity, asset, and talent that comes into your life. Be grateful for the good. Make the least of every handicap, setback, and loss. Accept the challenges, learn from them, and go on.

Third, we Christians struggle to accept the difficulties of the present because we tend to think that as God's children, there ought to be some kind of invisible shield surrounding us and protecting us. In our heads, we know the verse that says God sends His rain (and hail!) on the just and the unjust alike, and we're familiar with the story of Job, but in our *hearts* we cling to the idea that we should be exempt from pain.

After the great San Francisco earthquake and fire of 1906 had left the city in shambles, a newspaper reporter asked a good question. Noting that a liquor distillery was still intact, he wrote,

> "If, as they say,
> God spanked this town for being over frisky,
> why did he burn the churches down and
>   spare Old Hopalong's Whiskey?"

Isn't it strange what we choose to give God the credit for? Sometimes we have to accept reality without being able to explain it. If we could figure out everything God does or allows, He wouldn't be God.

When all is said and done, we're left with the fact that Christians, too, sometimes lose. And like everyone else, our happiness depends on how we respond to what life presents.

A few years ago, when positive thinking rallies were big events around the country, a friend and I decided we would get rich by putting on one of our own. We lined up speakers, rented an auditorium, and took out advertising. We had Jerry Clower, Paul Harvey, and Bob Richards speak, with Joe Dean as master of ceremonies. And to make a long story short, the people who bought tickets and came to the rally loved it, but there weren't enough of them, and my friend and I were left with a sizable debt.

We could have griped, criticized, and condemned ourselves and the people who didn't buy tickets. But when we were done with that, we still would have owed the money. We had to choose our attitude toward the experience. Bobbie really helped us keep everything in perspective. "If you can count your losses in money," she said, "you haven't really lost much." Not bad! We still had our minds, our health, and the love of God and our families. We hadn't lost much that was terribly important.

Learning to Accept

Even if you agree with everything that's been said so far in this chapter, you know that learning to accept reality isn't easy. I don't pretend it is. But there are a few things that are helping me to accept reality.

For one thing, time has a way of naturally mellowing most of us, and you may already be growing in this area if you stop to think about it. Can you accept some things today that you couldn't a few years ago? Give it a little thought, and make a list of things you couldn't stand last year or the year before but that you've now learned to accept. Then pat yourself on the back, give yourself a hug, and thank God you can still change.

For example, I used to be an easily irritated driver. A routine traffic situation would get me upset at people who didn't drive the way I thought they should. But I've learned there are a lot of drivers out there who will never handle a car to my satisfaction, and it's useless to get angry expecting anything different.

I'm also more accepting of young children's natural behavior. I didn't let our kids play with the stereo and TV knobs. But little children are naturally curious, and learn by exploring— and it really isn't too much effort to adjust the knobs again. So our grandchildren are allowed to explore and develop more freely. Recently when Amber, our granddaughter, was visiting, our son said, "Amber, your Daddy Tate is not the same man I grew up with." And he was right. And I'm glad.

Think back over your own positive changes in attitude, and you'll likely discover that you've already grown a lot in accepting reality.

Another understanding that helps is the realization that choosing to accept for now gives us power to change things that we don't get by complaining. In other words, accepting reality for the present doesn't mean you can't work to make things better, and it's the best way to bring about improvement. It allows you to stay composed, to evaluate life

---

If you can count your losses in money, you haven't lost much.

---

objectively, to make plans, and to carry them through effectively. On the other hand, if you're always complaining and just wishing things were different, you lose the objectivity you need, you tie yourself in emotional knots, and you forfeit the power to make real and lasting changes for the good.

This understanding helped me deal with the spelling problem mentioned earlier. For years I tried to conceal the fact that I was a bad speller. I figured that if everybody else could spell, I ought to be able to also, as if all I should need to do was snap my fingers to become a spelling bee champion. Of course life doesn't work that way, and it was only when I was ready to admit the truth—that I was a lousy speller—that I could quit hiding my problem and start improving. And while you would find it hard to believe if you read my unedited writing, I spell much better today than I did just a few years ago.

A third thing that helps me accept reality is the matter of turning frustrations into fascinations as mentioned in the preceding chapter. It's such a useful tool that I want to stress it again. The idea is simply that when you encounter one of life's many and inevitable frustrations, you choose to turn

84

it into an opportunity rather than allow your emotions to boil over.

Suppose, for example, that you arrive on time for a doctor's appointment, only to be told he's running almost an hour behind schedule. What do you do? If you're like I used to be, you sit there and stew and pout for an hour, flipping mindlessly through some ancient magazines and thinking the doctor ought to be paying you for the time you're having to waste there. None of that shortens the wait by even a minute, of course.

What could you do differently to turn this frustration into something useful? The possibilities are literally almost endless. You could ask the receptionist for a piece of paper and write a letter. You could go visit a friend in a nearby hospital. You could go to the library. You could make that quick run to the store that you hadn't thought you had time for. You could begin making plans for a date with your spouse. Weather permitting, you could take a relaxed walk. I always carry reading material with me and work on a future speech.

I could go on and on, but you get the idea. The fact is that in every frustrating situation, you may not be able to change what's frustrating, but you still have at least a few (and probably many) alternatives open to you. And as long as you have options, you remain in control of your life. You're still the one choosing what you'll do.

The frustrating thing about frustrations is the feeling that someone else has taken over control of your life. You feel that you are being forced to do something you don't want to do. Your plans are being shot down. But when you exercise your freedom to turn the frustration into a fascination or an opportunity—when you see you still have alternatives that aren't all bad—the frustration you can't change becomes a lot more bearable.

A final understanding that helps me accept reality is the idea that life is a journey, not a destination. As mentioned in the previous section, we tend to think just the opposite, dreaming about some grand and glorious day when all our needs will be met, all our problems will be solved, and we'll live happily ever after. Such a perspective feeds our discontent with the present and renders us unable to appreciate the good that's already in our lives.

The typical way we think is conveyed beautifully in a piece entitled "The Station," by Robert J. Hastings. It summarizes beautifully what I've tried to say in this chapter:

"Tucked away in our subconscious is an idyllic vision. We see ourselves on a long trip that spans the continent. We are traveling by train. Out the windows we drink in the passing drone of cars on nearby highways, of children waving at a crossing, of cattle grazing on a distant hillside, of smoke pouring from a power plant, of row upon row of corn and wheat, of flatlands and valleys, of mountains and rolling hillsides, of city skylines and village halls.

"But uppermost in our minds is the final destination. On a certain day at a certain hour we will pull into the station. Bands will be playing and flags waving. Once we get there, so many wonderful dreams will come true, and the pieces of our lives will fit together like a complete jigsaw puzzle. How restlessly we pace the aisles, damning the minutes for loitering—waiting, waiting for the station.

" 'When we reach the station, that will be it!' we cry. 'When I'm eighteen.' 'When I buy a new 450 SL Mercedes Benz!' 'When I put the last kid through college.' 'When I have paid off the mortgage!' 'When I get a promotion.' 'When I reach the age of retirement, I shall live happily ever after!'

"Sooner or later we must realize life is no station, no one place to arrive at once and for all. The true joy of life is the trip. The station is only a dream. It constantly outdistances us.

" 'Relish the moment' is a good motto, especially when coupled with Psalm 118:24: 'This is the day the Lord has made; let us rejoice and be glad in it.' It isn't the burdens of today that drive men mad. It is the regrets over yesterday and the fear of tomorrow. Regret and fear are twin thieves who rob us of today.

"So, stop pacing the aisles and counting the miles. Instead, climb more mountains, eat more ice cream, go barefoot more often, swim more rivers, watch more sunsets, laugh more, cry less. Life must be lived as we go along. The station will come soon enough."

Chapter Insights

1. Why is it so hard to accept reality?
2. Imagine you are in a slow-moving checkout line at the grocery store. What are some of your alternatives to getting frustrated?
3. What might God be trying to teach when your patience is tried?
4. What does Jesus say about mistreatment in Matt. 5:38-42?
5. How do we get the strength to choose the options Jesus called for?

CHAPTER 8

Accept Who You Are—Stop Comparing

Nothing is a greater impediment to being on good terms with others than being ill at ease with yourself.

— *Honoré de Balzac*

One of the excellent movies of recent years was *Amadeus,* which tells the story of Wolfgang Amadeus Mozart, the great composer. The film portrays Mozart as an incredibly talented man who chose to waste much of his life in debauchery. But the truly tragic figure in the movie was Antonio Salieri, a contemporary of Mozart's who narrates the story.

In the picture, Salieri was a man who devoted his life to music. As a boy, enraptured by the music he heard in church, he promised God that he would give Him his entire life if He would allow him to write sublime music. Salieri's prayer was answered. He wrote beautiful music, was highly acclaimed for his operas, and was chosen as the king's chief composer. His career seemed to be everything for which he had dreamed as a child.

Then one day Salieri heard the music of the young Mozart for the first time, and his world began to fall apart.

The problem was that Salieri immediately recognized that whatever musical gift God had given him, He had given Mozart a far greater gift. Salieri, the man who had given his life to music, compared himself to a genius and knew he was the inferior. Not only that, but the man God had blessed with the greater gift was also a moral degenerate. Why had God done this? Salieri was devastated.

Coming up second best in the comparison with Mozart led Salieri to two reactions. First, he railed against God. He believed that even though God had blessed him with great musical ability, He was now mocking him through Mozart for some reason. And Salieri would not forgive God this affront. Second, he became obsessed with a desire to destroy Mozart. He put his own career on something of a hold so he could plot to ruin his young rival's career.

By the end of the movie, we see how Salieri's envy of Mozart has made him into a bitter, frustrated old man who attempted to take his own life. He allowed envy to rob him of all joy in living, and it landed him in an insane asylum.

Now imagine another scenario. Suppose Salieri, rather than feeling crushed by Mozart's superior talent, had been able to accept himself and his abilities and remain thankful to God for them. What might he have accomplished? He *was* gifted by God, and it's entirely possible he might have left the world some truly great music instead of being lost in Mozart's shadow. But he cut short his own creative ability by constantly comparing himself so unfavorably with another.

The Big Negative

Comparing ourselves to others almost always brings about negative feelings. It's one of the surest ways to put yourself in a rotten frame of mind. It's at the root of all inferiority complexes. It can destroy relationships.

The negative feelings generated by comparison generally express themselves in one of two ways. Most commonly, they're expressed in false humility, where we feel and make ourselves out to be worse than we are. This was certainly Salieri's experience. And when this happens, we tend to become fault-finding critics, hoping that by tearing the other person down, we somehow elevate ourselves. The potential for this approach to destroy relationships is obvious.

The other way the negative feelings get expressed is in false pride, where we work at feeling superior to others in some respect so we can look down our noses at them. We see a perfect example of this in Luke 18, where a Pharisee

---

Negative feelings about ourselves and arrogance often go hand in hand.

---

went to the temple, noticed a hated tax collector (funny how some things never change!) who was also there, and prayed, "God, I thank you that I am not like all other men—robbers, evildoers, adulterers—or even like this tax collector. I fast twice a week and give a tenth of all I get" (vv. 11-12). Here again, the inherent power to ruin relationships is clear.

I've seen firsthand the power of false pride to destroy. Two couples come quickly to mind, and in both cases, the husband had a huge ego based on false pride. I saw these men give their wives the idea over and over that they (the wives) couldn't do anything right. As one of the wives said, "If anything goes wrong, I'm to blame." These men further conveyed the idea that their wives' needs and wishes didn't matter, and they would often humiliate their wives publicly through belittling. It was an ugly thing to see, and it's no surprise that both marriages ended in divorce.

The proper, healthy view to take of ourselves relative to others is found in Galatians 6:4: "Each one should test his own actions. Then he can take pride in himself, without comparing himself to somebody else." Sounds simple, doesn't it? Yet it's one of the hardest things to do.

The Bible doesn't stop there, however. For while we're not to compare ourselves to others, we *are* to be genuinely humble. God says we're all equal in His eyes, but we're to put the interests of others ahead of our own. This is the same attitude demonstrated by Jesus in submitting to death on the cross for our sakes (see Php. 2:3-8).

Based on observation and experience, however, I've come to the conclusion that we can only put others just a little bit ahead of ourselves. As much as we might want to obey the biblical command, we just can't seem to bring ourselves to honor others much more than we honor ourselves. So the lower we value ourselves by unfavorable comparisons, the lower we tend to value other people. On the other hand, if we're able to see ourselves as equal with others, we no longer have to put them down, and it becomes easier to honor them.

We see a negative example of this principle in the story of the prodigal son, told in Luke 15. Charles Hodge calls this chapter "the Bible in miniature." It pictures great sin and amazing grace in one short tale, and the major focus falls naturally on the prodigal son and the forgiving father. But there's one other major character in the story, the brother who stayed home.

When he heard his wandering brother had returned and Dad was giving a big party in the prodigal's honor, he first experienced the indignation of self-righteousness and self-importance. He went to his father and said, "Dad, all these years I've slaved for you. I've suffered the heat, I've worked out in the fields, I've done all the right things."

Could anybody disagree with those claims? I don't think so. He was in the right place, doing the right things with the right people. That's pretty good. So how *should* he have felt when his brother, who'd been out wasting his life and the family's money, came home and was greeted with the red carpet treatment?

He did the *natural* thing, which was to move into self-pity. "You never gave me a party," he said to his father. I don't think he really wanted a party! I think he had trouble with the truth. The problem wasn't a comparison of party versus no party but his spirit of bitterness and lack of love. Just because you stay in the right place and do the right things, like a Christian who faithfully attends church, doesn't necessarily mean you have a good attitude. The older brother compared the celebration over his sibling's return to the lack of appreciation he felt and couldn't find it in his heart to join in the joy of either his father or his brother.

Overcoming the Urge to Compare

The urge to compare ourselves to others—and to usually find ourselves wanting—is so deeply ingrained by our culture that it's extremely difficult to overcome. Society tends to compare and value us according to our beauty, our wealth, and our achievements, as discussed at some length in *Learning to Love*. And most of us come up losers by those measurements. Clearly, this is a system that offers happiness to only a very few, not to mention being contrary to the will of God. So how do we overcome this urge in our own lives? Let me offer four strategies that I've seen help others and myself.

The first thing is to choose a new and infinitely better standard against which to compare ourselves—the person and character of Jesus Christ. Make a study of His words and actions, His priorities and habits. Then ask yourself how you compare in each of those areas.

In 2 Corinthians 2:15, Paul tells us that we're to have the aroma of Christ in the world. We're supposed to "smell" like Christians. The problem, however, is that a lot of believers have "stinking thinking." They're mighty poor imitators of Christ, so they give off a foul aroma—not that of a Christian.

Now, it's easy to turn comparing ourselves to Christ into a negative thing. After all, He was perfect and sinless, so we're always going to come up short in comparison with Him, too. But unlike the world, Jesus loves us and accepts us completely even though He knows our shortcomings better than we do. So we don't have to feel defeated once we've confessed our sins to Him and received His cleansing (see 1 Jn. 1:9). Instead, with His loving encouragement, "let us fix our eyes on Jesus, the author and perfecter of our faith" (Heb. 12:2), striving to be ever more like Him. Rather than scaring or shaming us away, He becomes a magnet, drawing us ever closer to Himself, rewarding our loving faithfulness with His warm fellowship.

Bobbie and I had a class in our home for a while for "whosoever will" from our church, and a lot of "Wills" came by on Thursday nights. One of them was a bright, really great young man, but I sensed he wasn't at peace with himself. So one night I asked him, "Can you accept yourself?"

"No," he said simply.

"Why not?"

"Because I just can't. I'm not good enough."

"When do you think you'll be able to accept yourself?" I said.

"When I get better."

Talking further with him, I learned he was comparing himself to Christ negatively, falling into the rut such a habit inevitably creates. "Don't you realize," I said, "that when you get better in one area you've been thinking about, you're going to discover half a dozen other areas where you don't make the grade? How could you accept yourself then?" You can't ever win once you start that game. So sooner or later, if you're ever going to accept yourself, you've got to accept the way you are for now, just as He does—but set your eyes on Him as you continue to grow.

The second strategy is to make the other comparison that's helpful, which is to measure your present self against the you of yesterday. Are you growing, becoming more loving, more compassionate, more giving? Has your attitude toward life improved? If you can see progress—if you're moving in the right direction—you have cause to feel good about yourself and motivation to keep pushing ahead. The name of the game is becoming the best *you* can be, and if you're working toward that, you're on the right track no matter what anyone else says.

One of the areas where I would suffer from comparing myself to others is my public speaking. There are so many great speakers out there, and I could tell you which things the various speakers can do better than I. But it is much healthier to compare my ability to where I was one year or five years ago. Then I can appreciate the progress I've made.

A third strategy is to identify and develop at least one positive characteristic or ability you possess as a source of healthy self-esteem. Can you sing or play an instrument well? Then find some of the many available opportunities for using that talent. You'll have the satisfaction of feeling you've contributed to the lives of others, and you'll also enjoy their expressions of appreciation. Can you bake? Think of all the shut-ins, new neighbors, new mothers, and others who would be thrilled to receive some of your bread, cookies, cakes, or pies. Do you enjoy writing letters? There are countless friends, relatives, shut-ins, prison inmates, and others whose day would be made by a card or letter from you. Do you relate well to children? Your opportunities to influence young people for good are limited only by your time and energy.

A good place to start in the search for something in your life to develop is your spiritual life. God has given us all talents, and it is up to us to develop them.

> We have different gifts, according to the grace given us. If a man's gift is prophesying, let him use it in proportion to his faith. If it is serving, let him serve; if it is teaching, let him teach; if it is encouraging, let him encourage; if it is contributing to the needs of others, let him give generously; if it is leadership, let him govern diligently; if it is showing mercy, let him do it cheerfully (Ro. 12:6-8).

If you've never learned what your special talent is, your minister or Bible class teacher can help guide you in making the discovery and putting your gift to work.

This is also an area where parents can be of tremendous help to their children as they're growing up. Mom and Dad, encourage your little ones to try as many different things as possible until they find at least one thing they enjoy and

---

Accepting who you are gives you the power to become.

---

do well. Then do everything in your power to help them develop the ability. It will do wonders for their self-esteem and happiness in life.

For example, they may be able to excel in schoolwork, in a particular sport, in music, in art, in writing stories, in a game of skill (like chess), or in some kind of service to others.

Get to know your kids, and help them to find those things they can do with good results.

Our son, while an adolescent, developed an interest in taxidermy. And though it was a little inconvenient at times, Bobbie and I encouraged him in it. We paid for his courses, and stored his animal carcasses in the freezer. We also encouraged his interests in art and music, helping him to see he could do a lot of things if he really wanted to work at them. So did he become a professional taxidermist, artist, or musician? No, but he became a fine dentist, a profession that requires the kind of dexterity he developed doing those other things.

In the same way, we tried to support our daughter in her interests. In junior high school, she didn't make the cheerleading team the first time she tried, but we assured her she could be a great cheerleader. On her second attempt she was successful and the experience really bolstered her self-esteem. While in college, we encouraged her to participate in "Sing-Song" and "Summer Showcase," two musical programs. Now she's married to a songwriter (he wrote the intros to both of my videos) and she enjoys singing with him and to their two little boys. As she matured, she put her interests and positive self-image together to earn a degree in home economics and become a kindergarten teacher, and a confident, terrific mother.

The fourth strategy is to keep all promises and agreements with yourself. If you want to feel good about who you are and accept yourself, you have to trust yourself. Every assignment you accept and complete, every appointment you keep, and every exercise program you start and stay with makes you feel better about yourself. Such reliability also leads others to believe in you, which further bolsters a healthy sense of self-esteem.

On the other hand, every broken agreement and uncompleted task gives rise to more self-doubt that undermines your self-confidence. So work at being a person whose word is as reliable as the rising and setting of the sun.

By now, I hope you understand the futility of waiting to accept yourself until you reach a point where you feel you are good enough. If you're honest with yourself, you'll never reach such a point, because only perfection will satisfy that mindset. Instead, if you can accept yourself as you are for now, you'll find the freedom to grow and develop into more of what you want to be—and most especially, what you know God wants you to be.

Chapter Insights

1. Does comparing ourselves with others cause negative feelings? Why?
2. Why is it so hard to feel good about yourself even if you're making progress?
3. Do you tend to be harder or easier on yourself than you are on others?
4. Do you think that is right and helpful? Why?
5. Write Galatians 6:4 in your own words.

CHAPTER 9

Accept Responsibility—Stop Blaming

The ability to accept responsibility is the measure of the man.

— *Roy L. Smith*

One time a football team's starting quarterback was injured and had to be taken out of the game, and the coach prepared to send in his second-stringer. The team had its back to the wall. The score was tied, the ball was on its own six yard line, and the other team's defense was digging in.

Rather than risk a fumble in that situation with an inexperienced quarterback, the coach told the rookie, "Look, I don't even want you to hand the ball off. All you have to do is take the snap from center and run it up the middle three straight times, then punt. Do you understand?" To make sure he understood, the coach had the quarterback recite the instructions back to him.

So the second-stringer went into the game with his orders firmly in mind. On the first play, much to everyone's surprise, he found a big hole in the middle of the line and ran for twenty-five yards. On the second play, he went off left tackle for another twenty-five yards. On the third play, he broke a couple of tackles and ran all the way to the opponent's three yard line!

Then on the fourth play the quarterback dropped back and punted the ball out of the end zone.

When the second-stringer got back to the sidelines, the coach was yelling and jumping up and down and turning blue in the face. "What in the *world* were you thinking about when you punted that ball?" he screamed.

"Well," the quarterback said, "I was thinking what a stupid coach you are for telling me to punt on their three yard line."

There's more fiction than truth in that old story, but it illustrates beautifully a common human tendency—the refusal to take responsibility for our choices and actions and instead find someone else to blame when things go wrong. We see it every day in situations like the following.

"Why are you throwing your life away?" I asked a student who had an abuse problem.

The answer: "Since I never got to make any decisions of my own when I was home. My *mom and dad* made all of my decisions. Now I am doing drugs and drinking."

When I inquired of a student who seemed to be rebelling against everything good why he was choosing to react this way, his reply was, "Because all of my life I had to be the good child and the perfect student for my *parents.*"

"The reason I am the way I am is because I was born illegitimate of unwed parents. My *grandparents* raised me and never gave me enough love."

"I'll never be a Christian because my *dad* was a preacher and I hate the church and what it did to him."

"My *parents* moved all the time and I never got to settle down with friends, that's why I'm like I am."

"I was born into an *alcoholic family* of two generations and I am what I am today because of alcohol in my life."

"I'll never go to church again. The *people* were unfriendly and they ran me off."

The recurring theme in all these cases is the blame game, the attempt to shift blame with a convenient excuse. After all, who wants to take the blame when things go wrong or when someone is upset with you? Much better to allow someone else to be in hot water, right?

We're encouraged to indulge in the blame game by our modern culture. It tells us that accepting 100 percent responsibility for our lives is too tough. So blame somebody else. Take a drug or a drink. Cop out. And if something bad happens, sue.

When I was growing up in Alabama, I constantly heard expressions like "Just hoe your own row to the end." "Fly your own kite." "Pull your own little red wagon." "Stand on your own two feet." "Every tub sits on its own bottom." Though I didn't know it at the time, they were teaching me responsibility. Ultimately, everyone does have to answer for himself or herself.

The Circle of Self

Dave Grant explains responsibility by illustrating with a circle entitled "Me". That circle represents an individual. What part of an individual belongs inside the circle? What makes up who you are, besides your physical body? There's your spirit, your memories, your dreams and goals, your knowledge, your values, your will, your thoughts, your choices, your emotions, and your feelings. Do all of them belong inside the circle?

Of course they do, but you wouldn't know it to hear most people talk. "*He* frustrates me no end." "*She* drives me to tears." "*It* makes me so mad." (Have you seen an "it" lately? Does it have purple fur?) We talk about having anxiety attacks as though our emotions are running around out there

---

You can't feel better until you think better.

---

somewhere, waiting to jump on us while we walk down the street. In the same way we talk about not being in the mood for something. But can you imagine a guy's saying, "I believe I'll report to my job when I get in the mood"? No, we can control our moods when necessary. All the emotions are inside our circle.

What things are outside our circle? The events or situations or life, the environment, the government, traffic, other people, etc. (A popular song from years ago said, "I've got you under my skin." Can you imagine going around with someone under your skin?)

Now, here's the point: Even though we would like to blame our problems on something or someone other than ourselves, *nothing outside the circle can upset us unless we choose to allow it*. Events and circumstances and people certainly influence us constantly, but *we choose* how they affect us. *We control* our reactions and responses. Thus, there are no victims, only volunteers, in the game of life. Our chances of getting the world outside to satisfy all our wishes and eliminate all our frustrations are zero. But *we decide* what it all means to us.

A warm spring Saturday starts out sunny and beautiful, but then around noon the sky clouds over and the rain begins. Everyone in town faces the weather reality, but the reactions are very different. A man is frustrated because his golf game is rained out. His wife is happy, however, because now she can get him to do some work around the house. The teenager next door is elated because now he doesn't have to wash the family car. The couple two doors down are disappointed because their first barbecue of the season has to be postponed. These people have chosen their own reactions to the weather, and the fact that the circumstances didn't dictate their emotions is made plain by how different the reactions are.

At any given time, our emotional reactions to the world outside the circle of self are determined by what Dr. Maxie Maultsby, Jr., calls the ABC's of emotions. It's a three-step process. First, there's the event or circumstance. This is often something beyond our control, like an unexpected thunderstorm. Second, our minds evaluate the event based on *our* belief systems and values. Then third, out of our evaluations come our feelings. In other words, the way we *think* (evaluate) determines the way we *feel*.

We tend to think that there is just a two-step process—event causes emotion. The reason for this is that we've *programmed* in certain evaluations through repetition, and the mind produces them instantly in response to the triggering events. Thus, we no longer need to think through those evaluations; they come automatically, like a well-programmed computer.

For example, I programmed my mind a long time ago to evaluate the sight of a snake as a dangerous situation, calling for an immediate response of fear and flight. So I don't have to think about how to feel or act when I see a snake. I don't even try to figure out what type of snake it is or whether it's venomous or harmless. I just automatically choose to avoid the situation. It all happens so fast that it doesn't seem there's been time for any evaluation, but that's only because the assessment was programmed in years ago and has been reinforced through repetition.

Programming from the past can be changed, however. Jim Newman in his book, *Release Your Brakes,* gives another way to picture our power to choose as an imaginary horizontal line, with the words "have to" and "can't" at the left end of it, and the words "want to" and "can" at the right end. In the middle of this imaginary line are the words "decision" and "choice."

The more we move to the left of that center line in our thinking, the more negative we become, with phrases like "I ought to"; "I ought not"; "I hadn't better"; "I must"; "I want to but can't." If we move to the right of the center line, however, we can become progressively more positive using phrases like "I'd like to"; "I'd prefer"; "I'd enjoy"; "I'm capable"; "Excellent performance."

Although it varies from activity to activity, most of our lives are spent somewhere on the left side of that imaginary line. Our days seemed filled with "musts" and "shoulds" and "have tos." Suppose we imagine that only the right side of that imaginary line exists. In that case, we can only use the words "choice," "decision," and the positive phrases. Then what would your emotional reactions be to your work, other people, and your day's activities?

When I ask that in seminars, people say they'd be happy, contented, peaceful for a change, more productive and successful, and would feel better about themselves. You'd agree with that assessment, wouldn't you? Well, here's the good news. The fact is that the right side of the chart is really all there is because in reality we always choose between alternatives. The left side doesn't exist except as we conjure it up in our minds so we can feel bad and have something or someone to blame it on. In other words, unless you've been literally overpowered by threat or actual force, you've *chosen* to do everything you've ever done.

Since that's true, let me suggest that you begin to sprinkle your language with the word "choice" (or some variation of it). Start saying things like "I'm choosing to get angry"; "I'm choosing to let this traffic jam upset me." The great thing about admitting responsibility is that if you're choosing to be upset, you can also choose *not* to be upset. The power of choice is yours.

If something outside your circle of self were dictating your emotions, you'd be at its mercy, under its control. But since you *choose* to be upset, you can choose instead to be happy. Isn't that marvelous?

At this point, you're probably ready to point out some negative things that you think *do* control your emotions. Taxes, for instance. You "have to" pay them, and nobody likes paying taxes. But do you have some alternatives? The more alternatives we see ourselves having, the more we feel in control of our lives. So what are the alternatives to paying taxes?

For one thing, you could refuse to pay taxes and go to jail. That's not a pleasant prospect, but it is an alternative. Another would be to transfer your citizenship to a country where they don't have an income tax. A third would be to just not make any money from now on. They can't get blood out of a turnip, after all. Still another alternative would be to give away everything you make. That might free you from tax (of course I'm not a tax lawyer) and help a lot of people besides, if you gave to good causes. You could also cheat. I don't recommend it, but for some it works—until they get caught.

There you have five live alternatives to paying Uncle Sam (and there are probably others). Personally, I don't care for any of them. I don't like to pay taxes, either, but considering these alternatives, paying my taxes doesn't seem quite so bad. I'd rather do that than any of those other five possibilities. Therefore, I "choose" to pay my taxes. And if I'm the one making the choice, I can make it happily. Why not?

I explained all this to my college class once and concluded by telling them how happy I was to pay my taxes. A student responded, "You're crazy! You can't do that." (He thought it was somehow un-American to be glad to pay taxes.) So I said, "Look, if complaining will lower your tax bill, by all means complain. But the fact is you're going to pay the same amount regardless of your attitude." Why not choose to be happy about taxes, or any other situation you can't change?

People have used the loss of a job to embark on new, better paying, and more satisfying careers. They've used the tragedy of divorce to find better surroundings, new friends, and fresh hope for the future. Bad things do happen, and I'm not saying we should deny their badness. But we can decide to make something good out of even the worst circumstances. The choice is ours.

Unavoidable Responsibility

The Bible makes it plain that God holds us responsible for our thoughts, words, and actions—regardless of what modern society says. "For we must all appear before the judgment seat of Christ, that each one may receive what is due him for the things done while in the body, whether good or bad" (2 Co. 5:10). "Man is destined to die once, and after that to face judgment" (Heb. 9:27). "He [God] will bring to light what is hidden in darkness and will expose the motives of men's hearts. At that time each will receive his praise from God" (1 Co. 4:5).

We could go on and on quoting verses that show how God holds us accountable. From the beginning, however, people have been trying to escape their responsibility. You'll remember that in the Garden of Eden, after Adam and Eve sinned, God came walking in the garden and asked Adam what had happened. Adam said, "Don't blame me. Check it out with that woman *you* gave me" (my paraphrase). In other words, Adam had the audacity to try to shift his responsibility for choosing to sin onto God Himself. The implication was that if God hadn't brought Eve into his life, he never would have sinned. Don't believe that for a second!

However, God went to Eve and asked for her side of the story. She said, "I'm responsible. I admit it. The buck stops here." Right? No, she said, "There's a snake in the grass somewhere around here, and it's all his fault. Check with him." And as Zig Ziglar says, that old snake didn't have a leg to stand on. (Actually, I feel a little sorry for Adam and Eve, because they couldn't blame anything on their parents the way you and I do.)

The Lord, of course, would have none of this, and Adam and Eve had to pay the price for their disobedience, just as we also have to answer for ours.

Nor is our accountability to God the only reason we need to accept responsibility for ourselves and stop blaming. Another vital reason is that it's the only way we'll ever grow. Blame stops all growth. Why should I endure the pain of

---

There are no victims— only volunteers.

---

change and growth if my present sad condition is your fault? It's so much easier to keep blaming you. And if I pretend you control me—if you "make" me mad or don't give me the kind of love that I "feel" like reciprocating—I can blame you not only for my current condition, but also for my inability to improve.

The flip side of that is that to the degree you stop blaming, you also stop having negative feelings. It's like pulling the plug from the power source. Blame generates all kinds of bad emotions, doesn't it—bitterness, self-pity, defeatism, anger, and disappointment, to name just a few. You also can't forgive when you're blaming, and if you can't forgive you'll never have peace of mind. But when you pull the plug of blaming, all the power to those negative emotions is cut off, and life becomes a whole lot more enjoyable.

For Those with Deep Hurts

I know some of you reading this are suffering deep hurts. You might want to say to me at this point, "It's easy for you to say I should stop blaming, but you don't know what I've been through, what my parents [or whoever] did to me. I have a right to blame them for hurt I'm still suffering." Let me say a few words especially to you if this is your situation.

First, I certainly don't mean to make light of your pain. I know it's real and deep. Second, I don't intend to give the impression that learning to stop blaming and accept responsibility for yourself is going to be easy. It will probably be very tough. But third, you *can* do it, and you *must* if you ever want peace and joy in your life. There are four stages I believe you must go through.

You can begin by acknowledging you've been hurt, by facing squarely the reality of what was done to you. This is difficult and painful, I know. I've been told by people who were abused as children, for example, that their minds have shut out the truth of what happened for years, and that when they remember the abusive events, it can be devastating. Young minds blank out abuse, I think, as a kind of defense mechanism, a way of not having to deal with a reality that's too painful or too confusing.

The subconscious mind, however, doesn't forget. And until the truth is admitted and confronted, it continues to gnaw away below the surface. For this reason, people who seem to have all the elements of a happy life may suffer a chronic depression or recurring bouts of anger they don't understand. Getting the past hurt out into the open is the beginning of overcoming the problem.

Next, you have to accept reality. You don't have to like it, but you have to accept what happened. All the arguing and denial in the world won't change it. This is so hard because it may mean having to accept the fact that someone you love intentionally hurt you. It may mean having to accept that someone whose love you needed didn't actually love you, whereas you've been clinging to the fantasy that this person really did love you. Again, this can be very difficult.

Then you have to choose to forgive the person who hurt you. (This isn't getting any easier, but it's the only way out.) You don't have to feel warmth for, or like the person, although you'll feel better sooner if you do. Forgiveness is simply a choice you make in obedience to Jesus' command: "If you forgive men when they sin against you, your heavenly Father will also forgive you. But if you do not forgive men their sins, your Father will not forgive your sins" (Mt. 6:14-15).

A good test of whether you've actually forgiven someone is if you're able to genuinely ask God to bless the person. Again, you don't have to like the person. But can you sincerely ask God to fill the person's life with good? To the degree you can, you've forgiven. In time God will bless you with the ability to have loving feelings. More will be said about the need to forgive in the next chapter.

Finally, you need to be able to be thankful or to count your experience as a blessing. Can you, for example, see how your experience has made you a more compassionate person? Has it given you a desire to help the hurting? Are you able to minister comfort to others whom even professional counselors haven't been able to reach?

God has a way of bringing good out of bad, of making strength out of weakness, of turning our hurts into great blessing for ourselves and others. Look for those things in your own life. Let God use what you've been through to bless others. Then you'll know your suffering has not been in vain.

The process is not simple. And it may be something you can't do alone. So don't be afraid or ashamed to get help. Find someone with whom you can talk, someone who'll listen without judging you, someone you know will pray for you. And God will help you.

Moving Toward Responsibility

Owning up to responsibility for ourselves is a lifelong struggle. It takes real spiritual and emotional maturity. But there are three things that can help if we will practice them over and over.

First, when we trace blaming back to its roots, ultimately we blame either God or our parents for just about everything. "Why did God allow this to happen? Why did He make me this way? Why didn't Mom and Dad teach me better self-discipline? Why couldn't they see I needed more help in school?" So we need to search our hearts for the many ways we're blaming and confess it to God, and admit we're responsible people who make our own choices.

Second, we need to give thanks for the way we're made—especially for those features we most want to change. This can be absolutely life-changing, because if we can be truly thankful, we'll find either the power to change what we don't like or the grace to live with it in peace and joy. (See 2 Co. 12:7-10). More will be said about the need for gratitude in Chapter 11.

And third, we need to put ourselves back on God's spinning wheel and let Him mold us like clay into vessels fit and willing to give Him glory in His service. Then we'll be, as the apostle Paul wrote to young Timothy, "instrument[s] for noble purposes, made holy, useful to the Master and prepared to do any good work" (2 Ti. 2:21).

Chapter Insights

1. Why do people blame others for their shortcomings?
2. Do you have a problem or shortcoming for which you blame someone else?
3. Does blaming help to overcome the problem? Why?
4. Read 2 Corinthians 5:10. What is God likely to say about blaming others?
5. Why does growth stop when we blame others?

CHAPTER 10

Change Bitterness to Blessing— Stop Holding Grudges

Every man should have a fair-sized cemetery in which to bury the faults of his friends.

— *Henry Ward Beecher*

Imagine that a man comes up to you and wants to shake your hand and strike up a friendship. There's only one problem. He's dragging behind him a dead, rotten, stinking dog. "Would you like to pet my dog Fido?" he asks. "I know he's dead and he stinks, but he's my pet, and I love him. I just can't bear the thought of parting with him."

Needless to say, you wouldn't want to stay very long in that man's company. The stench of a dead dog is not at all inviting.

None of us would carry around a dead dog, of course. Yet many people drag something just as smelly with them wherever they go—the dead past, with grudges they've nursed for so long that they love them and can't bear the thought of letting them go. They won't turn the past loose, and they want everyone to pet the carcass, too, reassuring them that they were mistreated and giving them sympathy. It's a most unattractive picture, isn't it?

You probably know some folks like that. (It's hard to forget them!) But to some extent we all may be harboring grudges. None of them smells like Chanel No. 5, and carrying them around makes us very unattractive, not to mention making us miserable. So we need to change our bitterness into blessing and stop holding grudges.

For Ourselves

As already suggested, one reason we need to stop holding grudges, to forgive those who have wronged us, is for our own well-being and happiness. It's vital to mental, emotional, and spiritual health. Why? Because unwillingness to forgive poisons our memories, lowers our sense of self-worth and contentment, strains the relationship with the other person, and even blocks our communication with God (see Mt. 5:23-24).

Holding a grudge and allowing bitterness to fester can even kill you. Herman Melville's classic novel *Moby Dick* reveals this clearly. You'll recall that the great, white whale had crippled Captain Ahab, and from that point on, Ahab grew obsessed with destroying Moby Dick. Hatred twisted Ahab's personality so that he became cruel and consumed with his desire for revenge. Every waking hour was spent plotting the whale's death.

As you read the book, it becomes plain before long that the chief victim of Ahab's hatred was Ahab himself. His obsession had made him the most unhappy person imaginable. And in the end, it destroyed everything—the whale, the crew of Ahab's ship, and finally the tormented captain.

Another story from history further illustrates the practical importance of forgiveness. We're told that when Leonardo da Vinci, the great artist, was working on his famous "The Last Supper," he got into a fierce argument with a man just at the point when he (da Vinci) was working on the face of Jesus. This argument involved strong feelings, bitter words, and threatening gestures.

When the dispute was over, da Vinci went back to his work and picked up his brush. But much to his dismay, he found that his creative flow was blocked and he couldn't make a single stroke. At first confused, da Vinci soon realized what his problem was. He put down his brush, went and found the man he had offended, asked for his forgiveness, and then went back to his work. Then he was able to pick up his brush and continue work on the face of Christ without difficulty. Making peace gave him the freedom he needed to create great beauty.

Forgiveness isn't just a last resort—something we do only out of desperation when all other options are gone. Instead, it's a positive, joyful choice that gives us a chance to see ourselves not as victims, but as victors. Our antagonists and the world at large expect us to get angry and hold a grudge at the slightest provocation. But if we choose to stay calm and to forgive, we move from weakness to strength. We demonstrate godly wisdom: "A man's wisdom gives him patience; it is to his glory to overlook an offense" (Pr. 19:11).

For Jesus' Sake

Of course, our own well-being isn't the only reason to forgive. It isn't even the primary reason. Rather, the main reason to forgive is the recognition of our sinfulness and the realization of how much God has already forgiven us in Jesus Christ.

We're all guilty of countless sins against God, as the Bible (and our experience) makes abundantly clear. "For all have sinned and fall short of the glory of God" (Ro. 3:23). "We all, like sheep, have gone astray, each of us has turned to his own way" (Isa. 53:6). "There is no one righteous, not even one" (Ro. 3:10).

Because of our sin, we deserve only the wrath and punishment of God. Instead, however, by faith we receive His love and mercy through the sinless Jesus' death on a cross in our place, satisfying the Father's judgment. "For the wages of sin is death, but the gift of God is eternal life in Christ Jesus our Lord" (Ro. 6:23). "But God demonstrates his own love for us in this: While we were still sinners, Christ died for us" (Ro. 5:8).

When we stop and think about the debt of sin we owe, the terrible sacrifice God made to pay it for us, and the depth of His forgiveness ("As far as the east is from the west, so far has he removed our transgressions from us" [Ps. 103:12]), we ought to have all the motivation we need to forgive others who have injured us. Having been forgiven much, we should be ready to forgive much ourselves.

Jesus used an unusual incident to drive home this point. One time He had dinner at the home of a Pharisee named Simon, and while they were eating, a woman of the town who had been a notorious sinner came into the house carrying a jar of perfume. Weeping, she wet Jesus' feet with her tears. Then she wiped His feet with her hair, kissed them, and poured the perfume on them.

Seeing this, Simon was indignant. He figured that if Jesus were really a prophet, as He was reputed to be, He would know this woman's background and refuse even to let her touch Him, much less make such a fuss over Him.

Jesus knew what was going on in Simon's heart and took the opportunity to explain what the woman had done through a story. "Two men owed money to a certain moneylender," Jesus said (Lk. 7:41). One owed over a year's wages, the other a little over a month's wages. Neither man had the money to pay back his debt, however, so the moneylender forgave the obligations of both. Then Jesus asked, "Now which of them will love him more?" (v. 42).

Simon answered logically, "I suppose the one who had the bigger debt canceled" (v. 43).

After agreeing with that response, Jesus turned to the woman who had washed His feet and went on to say, "Do you see this woman? I came into your house. You did not give me any water for my feet, but she wet my feet with her tears and wiped them with her hair. You did not give me a kiss, but this woman, from the time I entered, has not

---

Focus on how much you have been forgiven.

---

stopped kissing my feet. You did not put oil on my head, but she has poured perfume on my feet. Therefore, I tell you, her many sins have been forgiven—for she loved much. But he who has been forgiven little loves little" (vv. 44-47).

With a heart full of gratitude for the forgiveness of her sins, this woman literally poured out loving service to her Savior, just as we should. The Pharisee, on the other hand, considered himself a pretty righteous fellow in little need of forgiveness. The truth, of course—as Jesus implied none too subtly—was that he was every bit as much in need and should have been on his knees alongside the woman.

Paul put this motivation in a nutshell when he wrote, "Be kind and compassionate to one another, forgiving each other, just as in Christ God forgave you" (Eph. 4:32).

The story is told of a man who was so full of anger, bitterness, and self-pity that it made him physically ill and put him in a hospital. At his lowest point, in wretched condition, he said to one of his nurses, "Why don't you just give me something to end it all?"

Much to his surprise, she said, "All right, I will." She went to the nightstand beside his bed, pulled out a Bible, and read, "For God so loved the world that he gave his only begotten Son, that whosoever believes in him should not perish but have everlasting life."

When she had finished reading, she said, "There. If you'll believe that, it will end it all." And she was right.

Why It's So Hard

Total forgiveness is hard work. It begins with the *decision* to forgive, although the feeling often doesn't come either quickly or easily. And one reason it can be so difficult is that often we think the pain is too deep to heal. The worst hurts in life usually come from those closest to us—a parent, spouse, child, or friend. And when someone like this inflicts an injury, it may seem easier to cut the person out of our lives, emotionally if not physically, than to try to restore a healthy relationship.

C. S. Lewis said that as a young boy, he was deeply hurt by a bullying teacher, and he struggled all his life to forgive the man. But not long before he died, Lewis wrote to a friend, "Only a few weeks ago I suddenly realized that I had forgiven the schoolmaster who so darkened my childhood. I've been trying to do this for years, and each time I thought I had done it, I found that it had to be attempted again. But this time I feel sure it is the real thing."

Most of us can identify with Lewis's feelings of trying to forgive. Deep hurts usually heal slowly. A genuine desire to see the offender blessed doesn't come easily. And a grudge nursed over time may become so familiar a part of our lives that it's hard to give up, even when it's downright unpleasant, like a dead dog tied around your waist.

Much to his credit, Lewis *wanted* to forgive the teacher, and he kept at it all those years until he got it done. I think that the *decision* to forgive—the willingness to struggle with it, even if you know you can't honestly feel like you want to forgive yet—is the essential beginning place. God will see that desire and honor it, giving you the grace to forgive even as He does. He *knows* what the pain of being badly hurt is like, and He knows how to forgive in spite of it.

A father whose soldier son had been killed in combat demanded bitterly, "Where was God when my boy died?"

His wise pastor answered, "In the same place He was when His Son was nailed to a cross for you and me."

Another reason it's hard to forgive is that our egos get wrapped up in an offense, and pride says, "Don't let him off the hook. Get your revenge." Well-meaning family, friends, and even fellow church-goers are likely to reinforce that attitude.

A man named Joe came up to me after one of my seminars in New Jersey and told me his story. His wife had gotten involved in an affair, he said, but because he loved her and didn't want to lose her, he forgave her and restored the relationship. His attitude toward the other man, however, was a different story. He just couldn't find it in his heart to forgive him. "I want to see him hurt the way he made me hurt," Joe said.

Joe knew that by holding on to this grudge he was hurting himself most of all. But his pride as a man had been deeply wounded, and the desire for revenge was powerful. And this greatly hindered his ability to forgive.

A Fresh Start

There is a humorous story about a man who stormed into

113

a newspaper office holding a copy of that day's paper. He demanded to speak to the person responsible for the obituaries, and was referred to a young reporter. With much agitation, he showed that day's column which contained his own obituary. "You can see that I am very much alive!" he complained. "I demand an immediate retraction." The reporter replied, "I cannot retract an obituary. But I tell you what I'll do. Tomorrow *I'll put you in the birth column and give you a fresh start!*" That's what forgiveness does—gives us a fresh start! We wipe the slate clean. We think and act as if the offense had never happened. There's absolutely nothing greater that can happen to a human being than to know he's been forgiven in that way by God or another person. Consequently, there's no greater gift we can give than such forgiveness.

One of the great doctrinal words in Christianity is "justification." And long ago, it seems, some wise person gave it this simple definition: Justification means God makes it "just as if" I'd never sinned. When He opens His ledger book of people's sins to my page (maybe "my chapter" would be more accurate!), He'll see a blank sheet except for these words: "Justified by faith in Jesus Christ." It's because we know God gives us this kind of fresh start that we want to do the same for others.

Jesus and Peter once had a conversation along these lines. Peter had just heard Jesus give instruction about making peace with someone who has sinned against you, and he wondered just how far this forgiveness thing should go. So Peter went to Jesus and asked, "Lord, how many times shall I forgive my brother when he sins against me? Up to seven times?" (Mt. 18:21).

Peter knew the Pharisees' teaching regarding forgiveness. According to reliable commentaries, you only had to forgive a person three times, and then you could take him down a notch or two if he offended you again. But Peter also knew that Jesus was more merciful than the Pharisees, so he proposed a number that was more than double the Pharisaic standard—seven, a number considered sacred by many ancient cultures, including the Hebrews.

Jesus surprised Peter, however: "I tell you, not seven times, but seventy times seven" (Mt. 18:22). Now, if you wanted to be legalistic, you could do some quick math and total 490 times that we're to forgive. But does that mean we're free to smash a nose after sin number 491? No, Jesus didn't intend that we should keep count at all. He was saying, in effect, that just as there's no limit to God's mercy toward us, so there should be no limit to our mercy toward others. Each time we're asked, we should be prepared to forgive and give the person a fresh start.

History provides many beautiful examples of the granting of forgiveness and a fresh start. King Duncan relates in one of his monthly publications that former Vice President Hubert Humphrey, shortly before his death, called Richard Nixon, his long-time political adversary who had already been disgraced by Watergate, to his hospital bedside. And then just three days before he died, Humphrey received a visit from Jesse Jackson. Why, Jackson asked, would Humphrey invite Nixon to his deathbed?

Humphrey replied, "Jesse, from this vantage point, with the sun setting in my life, all the speeches, the political conventions, the crowds, and the great fights are behind me now. At a time like this, you're forced to deal with your irreducible essence, forced to grapple with what's really important to you. And what I've concluded about life is that when all is said and done, we must forgive each other and redeem each other and move on."

Thus, in a moving, memorable scene at Humphrey's funeral, we saw the disgraced former president and long-time foe sitting in the place of honor. Mr. Humphrey, even in death, was giving a man who had been his great enemy a fresh start.

Another illustration comes from a common family on the other side of the world. Bob Conklin tells of a young Korean student who left his apartment to go to the mailbox. As he was returning, he was attacked by a gang of eleven teenage boys, who beat him to death.

Within a few days, the boys had all been arrested, and the community and the press called for the most severe punishment the law allowed. But then the authorities and news media received a letter from the dead student's family. They asked that the greatest degree of *mercy* possible be shown to the killers, and they said they were already raising funds for their rehabilitation. They added that they didn't want the boys to be hated and that they themselves—through a great strength of will, I'm sure—didn't hate the boys. They wanted their own boy's killers to be given a fresh start, an even better one than they'd had the first time around.

That surely is forgiveness after the instruction and example of Jesus, who from the cross asked the Father to forgive His executioners.

No Greater Message

The non-Christian world doesn't understand forgiveness. In fact, truly forgiving someone against whom you have a legitimate grievance may be the most unnatural thing a person can do. That's why the world doesn't understand, why we certainly need the Lord's help to do it, and why it's the greatest message of hope we'll ever have to offer. More than any other single thing, forgiveness indicates the touch and reign of Jesus in a person's heart. More than any other single thing, it sets Christianity apart from the rest of the world's religions.

When we know we're sinners, recognize how much and at what price God has forgiven us, and give that same forgiveness to others, there'll be a joy and excitement in our lives that's both noticeable and appealing. Our lives will become an almost-daily expression of gratitude to God for the change. And the first people to be affected will be our own families.

In a book titled *Christ and Prayer,* the author tells of a day when he was a little boy that his family gathered for evening prayer. Just before the prayer time, his father had discovered that a man he had thought to be a good friend, a man to whom he had entrusted the management of his property, had robbed him of all his estate. It was a crushing financial blow, one from which the family could never completely recover.

Nevertheless, the author wrote, in the family circle that evening, his father prayed lovingly and with understanding for the man who had betrayed him. The young boy was so

---

Forgiveness is a fresh start.

---

moved by his dad's spirit of forgiveness that he determined then and there that he wanted his father's faith.

Now, I ask you: was his son's salvation worth the cost of financial ruin? You know how that father would have answered.

Perhaps the most touching illustration of forgiveness I've ever heard came from Dr. Norman Neaves and involved a young clergyman in Illinois. This young man was sitting in his easy chair watching football on TV one day when the telephone rang. The caller was his sister. "Woody! Woody! You better come quick!" she said hysterically. "Something has happened to Mother!"

He ran out of the house, jumped into his car, and began the long drive to his mother's home, wondering and worrying the whole way. When he got there, he learned that someone had broken into her house and that his mother, seventy-three years old, had been beaten, robbed, and raped. She was swollen and bruised and at first the man just stared at her in shock. Then he ran to her, threw his arms around her, and began crying.

After a minute, as he was holding his mother, he smelled something strange yet familiar in the room. It smelled like chicken being fried. "Mother," he said, "what's that I'm smelling?"

"It's fried chicken, Son," she answered. "I thought you might be hungry after your long drive over here."

The man was so overcome by the beauty of her spirit even in such personal tragedy that he broke into tears again and squeezed her all the tighter. And then she looked up at him, her face aglow, and said, "Son, I want to tell you something, and I don't want you to ever forget it. God is still good! God is still good! God is still good!"

When the world hears a story like this, it first marvels at such a forgiving, loving attitude. And then those who are being led by the Spirit say, "I want a faith like that, too—something that will support me even in life's worst tragedies."

Eternity's Perspective

One more thing that's helped me to forgive is the realization that most of the things we get upset about aren't really worth the aggravation when viewed from the perspective of eternity—or even a thousand years from now. For so long I tried to be boss of the universe. Everybody had to march to my tune. I tried to get my favorite fast food restaurants to give me exactly the kind of service I wanted. I worked to get my bank and my students and (especially) my children to do things just so.

I have to tell you, though, that boss of the universe is a big job, and not an easy one. And once I learned to take the long view, I had to conclude that the job wasn't worth the strain, the wear and tear, that it demanded of me. Someone has said that you have just so much emotional deposit in the bank of life, and when it's used up, you're in trouble. Well, I had been using mine up fast for quite a while, and I didn't want to run out and die. So I resigned the position.

The difference that decision made can be seen in the way I treat students. When I still thought I was boss of the universe, if a student was late or was doing poorly in class, I took it almost personally and became angry. I also let the student know about it. But now I'll simply say to such a student, "I'm disappointed in your behavior, and do you know why I'm disappointed? Because you're special, and I love you. Come here and give me a hug."

Believe me, that loving, accepting approach has had a far better impact on both me and my students than my ranting and raving ever did. And it started with the adoption of a new, longer-term perspective.

Finally, if you're still holding grudges and you know God wants you to forgive, but you're afraid to let go, perhaps the following poem by an unknown writer will help you make up your mind.

> As children bring their broken toys,
> with tears for us to mend,
> I brought my broken dreams to God,
> because he was my friend.
> But then instead of leaving him,
> in peace to work alone,
> I hung around and tried to help,
> with ways that were my own.
> At last I snatched them back and cried,
> "How can you be so slow?"
> "My child," he said, "what could I do?
> You never did let go!"

Chapter Insights

1. Why are we usually slow to forgive?
2. In what way is forgiveness a positive option that we ought to embrace enthusiastically?
3. Read Matthew 6:14-15. Why does God place such a premium on forgiveness?
4. Mr. Tate also said, "Having been forgiven much, we should be ready to forgive much ourselves." Practically speaking, how do we keep the reality of our forgiveness in the front of our minds so we're ready to forgive others?
5. Is there a grudge you have against someone? What are the steps to getting rid of it?

CHAPTER 11

Be Grateful—Stop Complaining

*He who forgets the language
of gratitude can never be on
speaking terms with happiness.*

— *C. Neil Strait*

When I was in elementary school, my friends and I used to say, "Boy, I'll be happy if I can ever go to the bathroom without lining up. Wouldn't that be great?" When we got to junior high, we'd say, "Boy, I can't wait to get to high school." Once we got into high school, our line became, "I'll be happy if I can ever get out of high school." At that point, of course, we'd also say, "I'll be happy when I get some wheels" and "I'll be happy when I get a girlfriend."

Our assumption that we'd be happy at some later date when we got something we didn't already have is very typical, and it continues throughout life. Almost all of us play the game called "I'll be happy when. . . ." The pattern continues. "I'll be happy when I get into college." "I'll be happy if I ever graduate from college." "I'll be happy when I get a good job." "I'll be happy when I get a *better* job." "I'll be happy when I get married." "I'll be happy when I get divorced." [Check out the statistics.] "I'll be happy when I have kids—that will make me fulfilled." "I'll be happy when the kids are grown and out from under my feet." "I'll be happy when the kids are off to college." "I'll be happy when I get their college bills paid." "I'll be happy if the kids ever come home to visit." "I'll be happy when I retire."

We're always complaining it seems and never content with what we have. One time I asked a veterinarian what kind

120

of dog would make the perfect watchdog, and he started naming different breeds and the common characteristics they have that make them good watchdogs. And while he was doing that, it occurred to me that the human breed also has some common characteristics, one of the most obvious being our tendency to gripe. Unless we're careful, it seems to happen automatically as an innate part of our human nature.

We see the habit clearly in the Old Testament account of the history of Israel, whose people were expert at complaining. Read again the story of their Exodus from Egypt. Even though God had just led them to freedom, using many miracles on their behalf, they griped about the heat; they griped about the rocks; they griped about the food; they griped about their enemies; they griped about how long it was taking to get to the Promised Land; they griped about Moses' leadership (and by implication, God's)—the list goes on and on.

This attitude of ingratitude so infected the Israelites that when God had brought them to the threshold of the Promised Land, they refused to believe He really could or would lead them to victory. So finally God said, "Time out! Trip canceled!" He just called it off.

Do you see the power there? Their complaining and griping and criticizing bowled God over and caused Him to change His mind, so to speak. Now if it has that effect on God, what do you suppose it does to human beings? Few can handle it, and it's a major source of conflict between people.

The Quest for More

Behind our complaining habit is an insatiable desire for more. We've bought the idea—hook, line, and sinker—that the key to happiness is getting more, better, bigger, and newer things and relationships. Advertising and the mass media feed this notion. So we're off in search of more money, more prestige, more hobbies, new cars, the right clothes, more sex partners, the right perfume or after shave. We switch jobs, we switch houses, and we switch "significant others."

And when we get through, regardless of how much we've accumulated, it's never quite enough.

Why? Because if you're programmed to always want more, as sometimes we are, it's literally impossible to ever get enough. Do you think one year's salary in the bank would make you happy? If and when you get it, you'll find yourself thinking *two* years' salary or even three would be better. "Times are pretty tough," you'll rationalize, "so the bigger cushion would mean more security."

I know from experience that when a dreamed-of future arrives, it's never as satisfying as we'd hoped. By itself, it doesn't revolutionize our lives the way we'd hoped it would. As a basketball coach, all my life I'd wanted to go to the "big house"—leading a team to the national tournament. And one time I got there! But I discovered it's just more of the same. You put your pants on one leg at a time. The team gets suited up, goes out and perspires, and plays the game. The coach yells and paces the sidelines, working up an ulcer.

Then, before you know it, the tournament is over, and your life goes on just like always. And the realization that reaching this long-sought goal doesn't revolutionize your life leads to frustration and even depression. So what do you do? You pick out some other point in the future when you think you'll be happy, and you start playing "I'll be happy when . . ." all over again. It's called postponing happiness, and many do it indefinitely.

For instance, there are those who do it on a weekly basis. "I'll be happy when Friday comes" is their theme. Monday is typically a horrible, grumpy day for them, just something to survive. (If every Monday is like that, you'll have wasted over nine solid years of your life on miserable Mondays by the age of sixty-four.) Tuesday's not so hot, either. And on Wednesday they just kind of hang in there, because it's "hump day," which means that when it's over they're on the downhill side of the work week.

Thursday is not too bad, but only because their minds are now fixed on the weekend. Friday, of course, is only the lead-in to Saturday, when they'll really have fun. Saturday, however, often turns out with bad weather or to be a "Honey-do" day (Honey, do this! And honey, do that!). And

Sunday's not so hot because the preacher is boring, and besides, tomorrow is—Monday—and that starts it all over again. As they sang in the '60s, "and the beat goes on."

Breaking the Habit

How do we break this all-too-natural habit of griping? How do we stop playing the futile game of "I'll be happy when . . .?"One essential is to develop, with God's help, the attitude displayed by Paul in 1 Timothy 6:6-8: "But godliness with contentment is great gain. For we brought nothing into the world, and we can take nothing out of it. But if we have food and clothing, we will be content with that."

Food and clothing speak of the essentials of life, to which we might add shelter. But everything beyond that is privileges, preferences, and wants. And if we can learn to be content with the meeting of our needs, realizing that that is all we need to do the work of Jesus—which is where our focus ought to be—we can break out of the mindset of always wanting more.

It will also help us to reflect from time to time on how richly we have been blessed. Just by being citizens of the United States, we're blessed with the freedom to worship God without fear, to come and go as we please, to choose the leaders who will govern us and not worry that the losers will stage a coup.

Look at how blessed we are materially. The *average* person in this world lives somewhere in Asia and makes about $400 per year. He's not starving, but he's hungry, and chances are good his children suffer from malnutrition—that is, the ones who survive past the age of five. He'll never own a phone, refrigerator, car, or TV. He'll never live in more than a little shack, and he'll never know what a real vacation is.

We're all spoiled to death compared to the world average, and we ought to remember that and be grateful.

Furthermore, not only do we have the freedom to worship, but we also have access to the Bible and its teaching. We have multiple Bibles in every home, church buildings located conveniently and radio and TV broadcasts. But two out of three people who've ever lived have never heard the good news of the gospel. They don't even know about Jesus! Eighty percent of the people living today have no Bible and no hope of ever getting one. Let's praise God for the opportunities for spiritual growth that He's given us!

Whenever I think about things to be grateful for, I remember a young man named Keith Dunbar. He's been crippled from birth and can barely pull one leg in front of the other to walk around. It takes the same kind of effort for him to speak—the words come slowly and painfully. You can just barely hear him as he forces out a word at a time.

One day in class the students were telling significant events in their lives. When Keith's turn came, he stood up and said, "I've got such a great life! It's so wonderful to be

---

If our goal is to have more, we can never have enough.

---

a Christian and to be alive!" (Picture him straining every muscle in his body to get out an audible word as he said these things.) He went on, "How I enjoy watching other people use their bodies, and how thankful I am to be *able* to see other people use their bodies in athletic events and to do arts and crafts!"

Every time I think of Keith, I tell myself, "Willard, if Keith Dunbar, who'll never be able to do more than he can right now, can be thankful for being alive and for so many other things, how much more appreciative should you be?" Without a doubt, we have *much* for which to thank God.

We should also bear in mind that God *expects* us to be grateful, as He has every right to, and is displeased when we display an attitude of *in*gratitude. In 2 Timothy 3:2 and Romans 1:21, Paul listed some horrible sins of people who turn their backs on God, and prominent in both lists is a lack of thankfulness toward Him. Clearly, God takes the matter of gratitude very seriously.

If you're a parent, you probably can remember a time when you made a special effort to do something for your child, only to have the child seem ungrateful. If so, you can begin to know how God feels when we fail to give Him thanks. (If you're not a parent, perhaps you've received such ingratitude from a brother or sister, friend, or colleague.) Let's not be guilty of such sin but rather nurture this mindset: "Give thanks in all circumstances, for this is God's will for you in Christ Jesus" (1 Th. 5:18).

Privilege Vs. Right

A young lady in my college class suffered the sudden death of her father. As she spoke about it, she said, "No tragedy is unfair. The fact that God allows us to have relationships is a luxury." In saying that, she put her finger squarely on another perspective that helps us to stop complaining and be grateful. Namely, we need to see life's blessings not as rights but as *privileges*. I wrote earlier of our tendency to turn privileges into rights, but the issue bears brief repeating here.

Do I have a *right* for my good health, my good marriage, and a great career for life, without any bumps along the way? Or are those things privileges granted by God and for which I should be thankful? You recall what we said earlier about the average person on this planet and how much worse off he is than you and me. Why are we so favored compared to the great majority of human beings? Is it because we *deserve* a greater blessing from God?

No, the ground at the foot of the cross on which we all stand is level. We're no more deserving than the farmer in India or Uganda. The fact is we're greatly *privileged*, not richly deserving, and that calls for us to be appropriately grateful.

Charles Hodge tells of a church that needed some additional parking space. There was a vacant lot next door, and the church tried to buy it, but the owner wouldn't sell. "I'll tell you what, though," he said. "You can use the lot just as if it were yours—except for one Sunday each year, when you can't use it at all."

"Why can we use it only fifty-one out of fifty-two Sundays a year?" they said. "What's the point?"

In his answer the man showed great wisdom. He told them, "I want you to remember you don't own it." Every year they would be reminded of his grace, and also of their need to be thankful rather than take their parking privilege for granted. Whether they realized it or not, that owner was thereby doing them a great favor.

Enjoying the Moment

Believe it or not, I love to teach an early-morning class, because at some point during the semester, I'll take advantage of the time to make an important point. The students will come dragging in at 8:00 o'clock, their eyes half open, and I'll say, "Good morning! Let's start class by writing down twelve good things that have happened to you today."

One of them will answer, "Oh, Coach, we haven't been up but thirty minutes!"

"That's okay," I'll say, "write 'em down."

So they'll sit there for a few minutes and go, "Uh-uh," and maybe doodle a little on their paper.

After they've gotten comfortable (and maybe begun to think I'm crazy), I say, "All right, let's see if I can help you. This morning when you woke up, did you reach out and feel padded satin on all four sides? No? Then I guess you weren't in a coffin but were alive. Is that right?"

"That's right," they say with a chuckle.

"And is that good?" I ask.

"Well, yeah."

"Then write it down! Now, when you climbed out from under the covers and put your feet on the floor, you could walk, couldn't you? Is that good?"

"Yeah, that's good."

"Write it down. You *heard* the alarm, too, didn't you? You *saw* the clock telling you you'd better get a move on. And when you went in the bathroom, you got *water* just by turning the faucet handle, didn't you?"

One of them might say, "It was hot this morning! That's good."

"Write that one down, too," I tell them. "Now look. You've already got six good things that happened, and you haven't even been out of the bathroom yet."

What this exercise shows is that if we want joy and contentment in this life, we need to focus on this moment, this day, and look for all there is to appreciate about it. If we can't get excited about what we're doing today, tomorrow is never going to be any better. On the other hand, if we start looking closely, as the students do in this exercise, we can find all kinds of things to enjoy, to be glad for, and to get excited about.

The fact is that the only *guaranteed* time you have is right now. Yesterday is gone for good, and tomorrow is promised to no one. That's why the apostle James wrote, "Now listen, you who say, 'Today or tomorrow we will go to this or that city, spend a year there, carry on business and make money.' Why, you do not even know what will happen tomorrow. What is your life? You are a mist that appears for a little while and then vanishes. Instead, you ought to say, 'If it is the Lord's will, we will live and do this or that' " (4:13-15).

That passage doesn't say we shouldn't make plans—look again at the last part of it. There are many other biblical statements about the wisdom of preparing for the future. The passage does suggest that if you want to enjoy this life, you'd better put a lot into enjoying today, because whether you have a tomorrow at all is in God's hands, not yours. And we all have a lot to enjoy and be thankful for *right now* if we'll only look at it in the right way. The psalmist summed it up in a verse we all know but ought to take a lot more seriously: "This is the day the Lord has made; let us rejoice and be glad in it" (Ps. 118:24).

Maybe the best story I've heard concerning enjoying the day at hand is the following, which Ed Foreman tells about Judge Ziglar (Zig's brother).

There were twelve children in the Ziglar family in Yazoo, Mississippi. Their dad died when Judge was two and the mom and kids were left to scratch out a living from the Mississippi soil. At the time the story takes place, Judge was just a little boy not yet in school.

Every morning at 5:00, his mother would come to his bed, shake him, and say, "Son, Son, get up. It's gonna be a gooooood day today."

Judge says, "I'd jump up out of bed and run into the kitchen. Momma had a little milkstool with three legs, and I'd sit on it, and she'd throw a shawl around my shoulders and give me a cup that was half full of coffee and half full of milk. While I drank my 'coffee,' Mom would fix breakfast and get the other kids off to school. Then Mom and I'd go out and work."

On this particular day, Judge says, "I remember we were washing turnip greens, and boy, was it cold! It was so cold that the water had ice on the top of it, and I had to get a stick and break it." They had to wash and rinse the greens in that icy water, and by the end of the day, Judge's hands and arms ached all the way up to his shoulders. "I looked over at Mom and said, 'Mom, I ain't havin' no good day.' "

The next morning, Mrs. Ziglar came in at 5:00 as usual and encouraged Judge to get up. He continues, "I turned over and said, 'No I'm not going to get up—It's going to be a bad day.' " Mom just walked out and got the other kids off to school.

"About eight or nine o'clock, I came bouncing into the kitchen and sat down on my little three-legged stool. Mom said, 'What are you doing?' I said, 'Well, I got up to get some breakfast.' She said, 'Oh, no. You chose this to be a bad day, and it's gonna be bad all day long.' Then she led me right back to bed, where I stayed the rest of the day.

"Now," Judge goes on, "you'd think any loving momma would want to feed her son dinner [lunch]. But not my loving, disciplining mother. When dinner came, I just stayed there in bed. When the other kids came home from school and played, I didn't get to join them. And when it came time for supper, I still didn't get anything to eat.

"The next morning, just like always, Momma came in at 5:00, shook me, and said, 'Son, Son, get up! It's gonna be a gooooood day today!' I jumped out of that bed, ran to that kitchen, and sat down on that stool. And I've been getting up and being thankful every day since."

That was a hard way to learn to appreciate and make the best of each day, but it was a lesson well taught and well received. May we be wise enough to learn from Judge's experience and not have to miss too many meals ourselves!

One way to say all this is Psalm 118:24, quoted earlier. Another way is to say, "I'll allow no one to ruin this day." Our world is full of negative people and negative circum-

---

You can't live in rewind or fast-forward.

---

stances, most of which we can't control. But we can always control what goes on inside and how we choose to respond. So you might want to write on your mirror as a reminder, "I will allow no one to ruin this day." Then practice enthusiasm and practice turning frustrations into fascinations.

Someone said wisely that you're no bigger than what it takes to upset you. Ouch! That hurts, because it makes me realize that a lot of times I haven't been very big. You may be able to relate to this, also.

Can I Do This and Be Effective?

If you're a hard-driving, results-oriented type of person, you may be asking right now, "Can I really take this approach to life and be effective? I don't seem to get anywhere unless I get upset with people or the situation." We've been programmed to think we have to get upset to make things happen, but in fact we *can* still be effective, even without getting upset.

I'm not talking about becoming apathetic. Of course we can try to improve things! But while we're working for change, we can stay cool and accept things the way they are for *now*, giving thanks for what's good.

Not long ago, a student named Charlie came to my office, upset because he had received an F for the semester in my course. (It takes a lot of effort to flunk my class!) He wanted me to give him a WP (withdraw passing), which is kind of like an honorary discharge and doesn't have any negative impact on a student's scholastic record. The facts of the case didn't warrant a WP, however. Charlie could offer only excuses; he earned an F.

He became angry with me almost the point of physical attack, but I remained calm, collected, and in control. I told him I could not give him a WP, and explained the reasons why. I spelled out the facts, and concluded by saying, "I know it's embarrassing to get an F, Charlie, and I don't like to give F's. But you have to learn to accept the consequences of your decisions, and because I care about you, I want you to receive the grade you *earned*. I hope that sooner or later you'll thank me for helping you learn to accept responsibility."

Whereupon Charlie cursed the school and blamed his failure on everyone and everything but himself. He accepted no responsibility for what he'd done.

The next year however, Charlie enrolled in my class again. This time his attitude was 180 degrees different. His earlier anger and irresponsibility had vanished, and he applied himself responsibly. This time he earned an A. The chances are that if I'd gotten upset when he came to me requesting the WP, and matched him shout for shout, he never would have come back to retake the class. My influence on him would have been forever gone.

Happy Discontentment

Paul, the apostle, told us to give thanks to God in everything. He also told us, "I have learned the secret of being content in any and every situation, whether well fed or hungry, whether living in plenty or in want." (Php. 4:12). And I firmly believe that being thankfully content is a major key to happiness.

I also believe, however, that God made us to strive for goals, to achieve, to pursue, to become. It's part of our nature. A tree grows as tall as it can in the light and soil available, and we need to yearn and strive to become the best we can be. Translating desire into reality is what the first part of this book is all about.

So how do we reconcile that good part of our makeup that causes us to strive for excellence with the need for contentment?

The best answer I can offer is what I call happy discontentment. It's being contented for the moment with what you have and what you are without being permanently satisfied to stay in that condition. If you ever become fully satisfied with where you are, you're in big trouble. The proper balance is to be content for now, gratefully enjoying what you have while still reaching for your goals.

Whether you're able to maintain balance between desire and contentment depends on where you focus your attention. There are just two focuses to choose from. You can focus on the blessings and privileges you have and be grateful and contented. Or you can focus on what you don't have and complain and be unhappy. The amount you have doesn't change the focus—your attitude makes the difference.

Perhaps an old, familiar story will make the point best. A lady came to an old sage for advice. "O wise one," she said, "I've got my husband and my children, and we're all in this one-room shack, and it's so crowded. I can hardly stand it, but I don't know what to do."

"Do you have any chickens?" he asked.

"Sure I've got some chickens," she answered.

"Bring those into your room for one week. Then come back and see me."

At the end of the week, she came back spitting out chicken feathers. "This is horrible!" she said. "It's worse than before, and I don't know if I can stand it any longer! What should I do, O wise one?"

"You own a cow?" he said.

"Sure I own a cow."

"Bring the cow into your room for one week. Then come back and see me."

At the end of this second week, the woman came back in tears, at the end of her rope. "This is it. I've had it!" she sobbed.

The sage answered, "Let me tell you what you do now. Take the chickens and the cow out of the room, and come back and see me at the end of another week."

When she returned, the woman was absolutely radiant. "O wise one," she said, "I have so much room now! Everything's fine."

It's all a matter of *focus. A thankful spirit turns all it touches into happiness*—(Ron Willingham.)

Chapter Insights

1. Why do we tend to postpone happiness?
2. Do you know anyone who seems to make the most of each moment? How would you describe that person?
3. What are the dangers in postponing happiness?
4. How do we balance enjoyment of the present with the need to plan for the future?
5. How does a thankful attitude turn all it touches into happiness?

CHAPTER 12

Keep on Loving—Even When You Don't Get What You Expected

*You can give without loving,
but you cannot
love without giving.*

— *Amy Carmichael*

A tourist stood on a river bank, watching a lumberjack hook and pull out some of the logs that were floating by. After a while, the observer asked, "Why are you pulling out only certain logs when they all look the same?"

"They may look alike to you," the lumberjack answered, "but they're not. Most of these logs grew on the mountainside and were largely protected from storms. They're good only for lumber. I'm letting them go."

"And the others?"

"The ones I've pulled aside come from the top of the mountain. They've taken the brunt of storms and wind for years and survived. That means they've grown up strong and have a finer grain than the other trees. They'll be used for special work."

That story illustrates several important points we need to consider as we draw near the end of this book. One is that even if you follow all the principles outlined in the first section about how to get what you want, the fact is that sometimes you *won't* get what you want. You'll greatly increase your chances, but this isn't a perfect world. Things don't always go the way we expect or the way they should. Life includes lots of trials that tend to leave us feeling like a tree standing all alone on a mountain top in the midst of a gale. (Read the book of Job any time you're tempted to think differently.) We need to be prepared for those times if we don't want them to spoil our joy.

Second, however, the fact that we don't always get what we want and that we go through difficulties isn't all bad. God often uses our adversities to mold our character—to test and help us develop strength, to help us appreciate Him and what He's given us, to discipline us. If we respond wisely, we often find that a problem is a stepping stone to a blessing in disguise.

One day a truck driver hauled some clay to a landfill, and as he was backing up to dump his load, he made the mistake of going back too far. As the back end of the truck extended over the pit, the weight of the load lifted the front end several feet off the ground, and the driver couldn't pull forward. He also couldn't dump his load now for fear of having the truck tip over backward. He was stuck.

"Now what are you going to do?" his helper asked.

Easing out of the cab, the driver said, "Well, I think I'll grease that front end. I'll never get a better chance."

That's what I call making the most of a bad situation!

Twenty years ago my family was experiencing financial adversity. I was teaching and coaching basketball at a small but great little school back in Alabama. The pay didn't keep up with inflation, and occasionally there was no pay at all. As a result, Bobbie and I were as poor as Job's turkey. (We had to lean up against the fence to gobble!)

Obviously, I needed more income to supplement my salary, and I looked for ways to earn more. I bought a distributorship for selling self-improvement programs which wasn't my first choice of a way to make a living, but I had no long-range goals in mind at that time. I was just acting out of financial necessity.

Because of that venture, however, I began to study self-improvement, attitudes, and human motivation. I found I enjoyed that study, so I stayed with it. And I began to read about the lives of successful men. And lo and behold, the writing and speaking I'm doing today that I enjoy so much grew directly out of that beginning. I might never have done it if it hadn't been for the blessing of adversity—my money troubles.

No Lack of Models

Many books could be filled with the stories of people who not only overcame adversity but grew as a result of it. For instance, George Frederick Handel, in 1741 seemed a broken man, he was paralyzed on his right side and could hardly hold his pen. His money was gone, and his creditors were threatening to imprison him. His wife had just died. Handel sank so deep into depression that he found himself wondering if he should throw himself into the Thames and drown.

Yet in those dark hours, he drew on a deep love for and faith in God, and he found reserves he hadn't known he possessed. And out of his fiery trials came some of the greatest music the world has ever known, including the beautiful, harmonious tones of praise of "The Messiah," which he wrote that same fall. Can you imagine Handel's feelings as he transcribed such biblical words as "Worthy is the Lamb that was slain to receive glory and honor and power"?

In the Bible itself, we have the story of Joseph. A young man when sold into Egyptian slavery by his jealous brothers, he suffered the loss of his freedom, separation from the love of his father, the defaming of his character, and imprisonment for a crime he didn't commit.

Yet years later, when he had matured into a great man of God and ascended to the right hand of Pharaoh, he told his brothers, "Do not be distressed and do not be angry with yourselves for selling me here, because it was to save lives that God sent me ahead of you. . . . So then, it was not you who sent me here, but God. He made me father to Pharaoh, lord of his entire household and ruler of all Egypt" (Ge. 45:5,8).

Out of great trial men are refined for God's use.

Certainly our greatest model of experiencing victory even in difficulty is Jesus Himself. He was misunderstood, constantly harassed by His enemies, rejected by friends, beaten and crucified, and made to bear the sins of the world. Yet He never stopped loving. He never lost sight of His goal, and in the end He won the ultimate victory over death on our behalf.

The Test of Love

Throughout this book, I've been encouraging you to love life—to establish healthy priorities that emphasize relationships, to set and pursue goals, to appreciate and make the most of each day, to forgive and reach out to others in love. It's relatively easy to do those things when life is treating you well. When the sun is shining and everything's going your way and you're getting what you want, it's simple to love everybody. At times like that, you don't need this or any other book to be happy.

The real test of love comes when you *don't* get what you want or expect, when life gives you only the pits and not the cherries. Can you still love then? Can you still find things for which to be thankful to God? Do you feel deserted by Him, or do you draw closer?

Our natural tendency is to fail the real test of love. That's human nature. And that's why in times of disappointment or trouble we need to turn up, or accelerate, our love.

Suppose, for example, that you work long and hard on a project at work, and it turns out well, but that at the last minute, a co-worker manages to steal the credit. Can you still love that person? What does it depend on? It would have to depend on us, and not that person's behavior. Most of us, in order to love someone, have to like everything about the person—so we do very little loving.

Remember that nothing outside your circle of self can control you unless you let it. So would you let this person, who doesn't deserve your love, make you into an unloving, unhappy person? If you become bitter toward someone, even if your bitterness is "justified," you'll never be happy.

What we want to try to develop is the kind of love that's not a barter agreement. The only way to peace and happiness is to say to others, including a cheating co-worker, "I love

136

you no matter what you say or do, no strings attached, no exchanges, no bookkeeping. I love you simply because you're special to God, who loves you every bit as much as He loves me. I may not like you, and I surely don't like some of the things you do, but I'll always love you and act in your best interests."

Is that hard? You bet it is. It's hard enough with family members who love you, let alone backstabbing co-workers. But because God commands us to do it—Jesus told us, for instance, to love our enemies (see Mt. 5:43-48)—we know that if we're willing, He'll provide the needed resources through His Word, His people, and His Spirit. He didn't command us to *feel* loving but to *act* loving or in the best interest of our enemies.

Perhaps it will also help us to bear in mind that what we give to others we're also giving to ourselves. Paul wrote the Philippian Christians and thanked them for their financial

---

Listening is loving.

---

support of his ministry. Then he added, "Not that I am looking for a gift, but I am looking for what may be credited to your account" (Php. 4:17). In other words, in giving to Paul, they were giving to themselves.

We've all known the Golden Rule from childhood: "Do unto others as you would have them do unto you." When you love others, you get love back in return. When you reject them, they reject you. The world is like a giant mirror in that respect—it reflects back whatever we send out.

Perhaps you've heard the story about the mountain climber who was overtaken suddenly by a snowstorm. His body quickly started to grow numb, and he knew he was in serious danger of freezing to death. Scrambling for safety, losing strength fast, he tripped and fell. Inspecting the object that had caught his foot, he discovered it was another person lying in the snow, almost frozen.

The climber began to massage the other person, trying to bring him back to life and get him to shelter. As you might have guessed, by working to save the other person, the climber saved his own life.

A mother asked her young son to take a bouquet of flowers to a shut-in who lived down the street. He did so, had a marvelous visit, and walked back home. When he got there, his mother asked him to smell his hands. Curious, he sniffed his little hands, and he was surprised to discover the fragrance of the flowers still lingered there. His wise mother told him, "Love always leaves a sweet fragrance."

How to Love Others

If accelerating our love is the way to be happy in difficulty and disappointment, how do we go about it? My first book, *Learning to Love* is devoted to that topic, but let me briefly suggest four ways to show love. Together, appropriately, they make up the acronym L-O-V-E.

First, learn to *listen*. If you give me your time, life's most precious commodity, and listen to me, you're saying you love me.

It was said of a great linguist that he could be silent in seven languages. But it's difficult to do it in just one, isn't it? Really, listening is the most challenging part of communication. It's been said that we wouldn't listen at all if we didn't know it was our turn to talk next. Ever tune someone out because you were thinking about what you wanted to say?

"Be quick to listen, slow to speak," James wrote (Jas. 1:19), but too often we get those reversed and we're quick to speak and *slow* to listen. And though I've rarely needed to repent of something I didn't say, I've had to repent of a lot of things I wish I hadn't said.

To be a good listener, you have to *want* to be one. Not many people want to listen, as a junior college proved. It offered a night course in listening and another in speaking. To meet the demand, they had to open up a second class in speech, but the class in listening was canceled because no one signed up.

Good listening also requires that you act the part. Lean toward the speaker and nod in agreement occasionally or say "Uh huh" from time to time. Maintain eye contact. Repeat back what the person said once in a while so that you both know you understand.

People today, especially children, are crying out for someone to listen to them. It's a great way to show love.

Second, learn to *overlook* faults. Close your eyes to a person's minor shortcomings. Forgive petty insults. We all make lots of mistakes; let's be kind to one another and not make federal cases out of them. "Above all," Paul wrote, "love each other deeply, because love covers over a multitude of sins" (1 Pe. 4:8). This is what we want others to do for us, isn't it?

How do we develop this attitude of love? Try to understand the other person a little. Since my wife is normally a loving person, I know that if she's a little snappy one day, there must be a reason. If I keep that in mind, it's easier to be forgiving. It also helps to know that before long I'll need her to forgive me!

Taking the long view is another help. If the members of a committee on which you have served are thanked by name, and yours happens not to be mentioned, how do you react? Oftentimes, we blow it all out of proportion, feel hurt, go home and sulk. But in the stream of eternity, it's not a big deal. It doesn't even register on the scale. So the long view really gets things in proper perspective—God's perspective.

And then, of course, we need to hate the wrong but not the person. Separating a person from his undesirable actions is one of the most difficult things we can ever try. It's a lifelong struggle, but don't give up. Just keep working at it. And to the extent that we can do it, overlooking and forgiving become that much easier.

Third, learn to give people *value*. Communicate acceptance. Make it clear that you love people and use things, not the other way around. Work to show appreciation to those who help you in any way.

You want something that will change you life? Make a list of all the people who have blessed you and helped you in the course of your life. You should come up with maybe forty or fifty people who've prayed for you, taught you, corrected you, helped you develop a skill, or whatever. Then one by one, locate those people and tell them, either in person or in a letter, how valuable their help has been to you. Your life will be richly blessed.

Early every semester, when my students are telling the class a few things about themselves, I pass out little square slips of paper. Then, after each student finishes his story, I have the rest of them write on a slip, "I like" or "I appreciate *(the student's name)* because. . . ." When they're finished they pass them in.

At the end of the hour, I distribute the notes to the respective students. Depending on the size of the class, they get thirty or thirty-five little squares stating something their classmates like about them. Sometime later, I'll ask them, "What do you do with your 'I likes'? Throw them away?"

"No, no, Coach," they say. "We read 'em over and over."

They know those notes weren't written voluntarily—each of them wrote as many as he or she received. Yet they've received so few such affirmations in their lifetimes that they eat them up. Imagine how they—or anyone else—would appreciate *unsolicited* affirmations.

Fourth, learn to give *encouragement*. A friend of ours named Suellen Phillips relates a true story from an older teacher about a little guy who in first and second grade had been bad news. His reputation preceded him to the next grade, and the teacher dreaded to see him coming into her class. She said to herself, *I've gotta do something to get him on my side. Maybe I can ask him to help me by showing some new students around the school.* She told him how happy she was to have him in her class and that she looked forward to having him as her helper.

Sure enough, the boy responded to the encouragement and tried hard to please his wise teacher. And one day as he was walking down the hall, he ran into the principal, who said, "Say, where've you been? I haven't seen you in my office lately."

"Shh," the boy said, "my teacher thinks I'm good."

That boy ended up being the mayor of Nashville, Tennessee.

Not long ago, the government did an expensive, three-year study of how to motivate workers. What they found was that the most motivational sentence you can use is this: "I know you'll do a good job." That's love, value, and encouragement all wrapped up in one.

There are a lot of philosophies you can live by. "This is the first day of the rest of my life" is a great one. The only problem is that it assumes I'm going to have some more life, and that is uncertain. So there is a better philosophy.

Try this one. "I'm going to treat each person I meet as if this is his last day." Think about that. How would such a perspective change what you say to people? The way you respond to them? Wouldn't you want to cheer them up, encourage them, send them on their way with a smile?

There's great power in encouraging words, or even just a comforting presence. A little girl came home late one day, and her mother said, "You're late. Where have you been?"

"Oh, my girlfriend's dolly's arm fell off," she answered.

"Did you help her put it back on?"

"No," she said, "but I helped her cry."

An anxious heart weighs a man down, but a kind word cheers him up. (Pr. 12:25).

Start Now

One of the best ways the devil deceives us these days is in regard to "quality time." People who are busy, with a lot of demands on their time, are drawn to the idea because it holds out the hope that you can have a healthy relationship without spending much time on it as long as the time you do give is "quality time." But the unavoidable fact is that you can't have quality time if you don't have some *quantity* of time. It just doesn't work.

There's a song that's become a modern classic called "Cat's in the Cradle." In it the writer, Harry Chapin, told of a father who never had time for his adoring son. When the son was grown and the father was old, however, the father wanted to spend time with his boy. But the son had learned to be just like his dad—too busy for a meaningful relationship. And then, too late, the father realized the consequences of his busyness.

My point is that if you want happiness, start turning up your love now. Don't wait until you can do it perfectly. Don't wait until your schedule clears up and it's conven-

---

Treat each person as if this is his last day.

---

ient. Don't wait for the other person to make the first move. Commit yourself to giving the time to really love the people in your life—to listen, overlook, value, and encourage them.

Legend has it that in 1916, George Gipp was tossing a baseball with a friend near the Notre Dame football practice field, and out of nowhere a football flew over and whacked him on the head. Gipp calmly picked up the offending pigskin and kicked it seventy yards in the air back to Coach Knute Rockne. Quite impressed, Rockne convinced Gipp to try out for the team.

The Gipper became a tremendous football player. He was a fast runner and a great kicker, and he won big games for the Irish.

As the 1920 football season was ending, Gipp had contracted pneumonia and strep, and he lay dying in a hospital bed. As Rockne hovered at Gipp's bedside, the Gipper muttered these heroic words: "Sometime, Rock, when the team is up against it, when things are going wrong and the breaks are beating the boys, tell them to go in there with all they've got and win just one for the Gipper."

Eight years later, the Irish were locked in a bitter battle with Army in New York. Eighty-thousand screaming fans were jammed into a stadium built for 75,000. The score was tied at halftime, and team spirits were low.

Rockne knew it was time. As the players gathered in the locker room for the halftime talk, Rockne took them back to that hospital room where the Gipper uttered those immortal lines to future generations of Irish athletes. As Rockne spoke, tears began to cover the dirty cheeks of the players, and a wave of fresh power swept over the squad.

When Rockne concluded with his famous line "Let's win one for the Gipper!" the team burst into a roar, tore onto the field, and rolled on to victory.

It's amazing, isn't it, what the memory of one great man can inspire others to do. Now remember that the one *great* man wasn't a mere football hero, but the Son of God who said His disciples would be known by their love for one another (Jn. 13:25). Doesn't that inspire us to love others?

Chapter Insights

1. How do we typically respond to not getting what we want?
2. How does our ability to love affect our responses to adversity?
3. What are four ways to show love? What can you do to improve your ability to love?
4. Read 1 John 3:16-24. What does this passage say about continuing in love in the face of adversity?